What Readers Ar
The PhD

"I highly recommend *The PhD Jou*
program or considering entering one. It would also ᵁᵁ
resource for PhD students' spouses and family members to read so
they can understand their loved one's journey and how best to support
them. I applaud Dr. Ngetich for sharing her experiences and wisdom
so the road can be a little smoother for those who follow her."

— Tyler R. Tichelaar,
PhD and award-winning author of *The Gothic Wanderer*

"If you are the first in your family and/or community to tackle a PhD
journey in a country a long way from home, this book is a 'must-read.'
You will discover how the author, through sheer perseverance
and intense determination, succeeded at one of the world's top
universities. Her practical advice, down-to-earth perspective, and
personal stories will inspire, motivate, and enlighten you towards your
own doctoral success."

— Susan Friedmann, CSP, International Bestselling Author of *Riches in
Niches: How to Make it BIG in a small Market*

"This book is an excellent resource for anyone contemplating or
committed to a PhD. It offers practical insights into the dos and
don'ts based on the experience of an academic and scholar who can
speak with authority and certainty on the subject. Dr Ngetich utilises
her story of perseverance, endurance, and overcoming the odds to
produce a tool that will enrich others. I highly recommend *The PhD
Journey: Strategies for Enrolling, Thriving, and Excelling in a PhD
Program* to aspiring and existing PhD scholars and PhD advisors."

— Ndjodi Ndeunyema, PhD in Law, Oxford University, PhD thesis
awarded the inaugural Subedi Prize for Best Law Doctoral Thesis 2019-20

"Africa needs more than a million scientists to move the needle on our development targets. Dr Ngetich's book combines her scientific expertise, a network of scholars, and practical experiences to provide a very resourceful book for the next generation of PhD students. A very timely and much-needed intervention for all aspiring doctoral students."

— Anne Makena, DPhil Chemical Biology, University of Oxford

"I have had the pleasure of watching Dr Ngetich thrive throughout her PhD journey. This book is more than a testimony of that success; it is the kind of guide I wish I'd had as I began my own PhD journey. This book will provide you with the confidence you need to enter and make it through a PhD, or even decide to find an alternative path. I highly recommend this book to anyone considering a PhD."

— Miriam Jerotich Kilimo, PhD

"As one who is contemplating pursuing a doctorate, I found that this book served as the guide I really needed. I appreciate the candidness with which Dr Ngetich writes. Her authenticity in outlining the ins and out of what a PhD journey will entail is exactly what anyone weighing the options of further study needs."

— Ruth N. Nyakerario

The PhD Journey

Strategies for Enrolling, Thriving, and Excelling in a PhD Program

Gladys Ngetich, PhD

AVIVA
PUBLISHING
New York

The PhD Journey:
Strategies for Enrolling, Thriving, and Excelling in a PhD Program

The resources and advice included in this book are provided for informational purposes only and should not be used to replace the specialised training and professional judgement of a health care or mental care professional. Neither the author nor the publisher can be held responsible for the use of the information or suggestions provided within this book. Consult a trained professional before making any decision regarding the treatment of yourself or others.

Paperback ISBN: 978-1-63618-174-5
Library of Congress Control Number: 2022902337

Edited by Dr Tyler Tichelaar
Cover art and interior layout by Meredith Lindsay
Illustrations by Sindhu Majeti
Foreword by Dr Priyanka Dhopade

Published by:
Aviva Publishing
Lake Placid, NY 12946
518-523-1320
www.avivapubs.com

Address all inquiries to:
Dr Gladys Chepkirui Ngetich
(www.gladyschepkirui.com)

Dedication

In loving memory of my late brother, Joash.

Contents

Foreword

I first met Gladys in 2015 when she had just begun her PhD at the University of Oxford. I was working as a postdoctoral researcher in the same research group. We had very few women researchers in the group, and I remember how excited I was to see the first Black woman join the group. But I could not imagine Gladys's thoughts as she embarked upon this journey in a new place, so far from home, where hardly anyone resembled her.

As I came to know Gladys better over the years, I felt inspired by her abilities and perspectives, whether as a competitive athlete or as an academic presenting at international conferences. I saw how strong and brave she was, but not until I read *The PhD Journey: Strategies for Enrolling, Thriving, and Excelling in a PhD Program* did I understand her empathy and deep commitment to service.

If you, like Gladys and me, come from a background where you will be the first in your family or community to undertake a PhD, then this book is especially for you. Gladys has thoughtfully compiled every single thing you may need to know before, during, and even after your PhD. Her voice is that of an older friend or sibling, someone who has been through it all and is looking out for you. Looking back, I wish I had read a book like this before I began my own PhD.

From the more practical considerations of choosing a PhD topic and advisor to the more intangible lessons on inspiration and motivation, Gladys provides useful insight, resources, and advice for every scenario. In each chapter, Gladys weaves through anecdotes from her own experiences and shares vulnerabilities that will make you feel close to her. While reading Chapter 4.13, "Be Kind to Yourself," I shed tears over the loss of her brother and the profound impact it had on her life.

This book serves as a reminder that a PhD really is a journey: an enthralling, at times frustrating, but ultimately rewarding journey. And it's a journey that takes place alongside our "real lives"—the relationships, life changes, and world events that can shape our outlooks as we pursue new knowledge during our PhDs and discover new aspects of ourselves.

Let Gladys' knowledgeable and compassionate words guide you through this journey. If she and I can do it, so can you.

Dr Priyanka Dhopade
Researcher and Lecturer
University of Auckland, New Zealand

Introduction

The first time I heard the word "PhD" was during one of my mom's vehement lectures about the importance of education. My parents always encouraged my siblings and me to climb the academic ladder. It would take another ten years before I would finally engage with the word PhD. That happened when a classmate suggested I consider enrolling directly in a PhD program after winning the Rhodes Scholarship. While their suggestion was enticing, the whole prospect of pursuing a doctorate crippled me with fear. After umpteen sleepless nights, I made the scariest decision of my academic life: to transition from an undergraduate degree at a relatively small university in Kenya to an elite institution abroad to pursue a PhD in engineering. As I prepared to embark on my PhD journey, I constantly questioned whether I had bitten off more than I could chew.

To say the University of Oxford was intimidating is an understatement. Floodgates of insecurities threatened to destabilise me, especially in the beginning. Most of the time, I wondered if I was the only one who felt intimidated and insecure. Everyone around me seemed to know exactly what their research was about. They seemed to have their ducks in a row. Being a minority in my lab only exasperated the already bleak situation.

Outside Oxford, I barely knew anyone in my closest circle who was in the same turbulent PhD boat as me. Whenever the school brochures couldn't answer my endless questions or respond to my list of worries, I tried the internet, which helped only sometimes. Some questions were as simple as: Which PowerPoint template or reference management software should I use? Some questions, however, didn't have an immediate or direct answer. Questions like: Am I in the right place? Is the PhD the best route for my career? What exactly do I need to do to earn a PhD? Will the dark clouds of fear and imposter syndrome ebb away? Are the insecurities I occasionally feel unique only to me, or do other students experience them too? What are some of the best strategies and practices to thrive in the PhD journey? A list of other endless questions and worries riotously criss-crossed my mind.

I wish I could tell you that this maze of questions will only emanate from within you, but sometimes, these questions will come from people around you. The question "How is your research coming along?"—as innocent as it may sound—is always dreaded by a PhD student. It immediately reminds you of failed experiments, failed computer simulations, failed fieldwork, failed results validations, and rejected papers. This question has an invisible power to transform your mood instantly from a beaming party mood to a depressed one. It is an unwritten rule never to ask a PhD student how their research or thesis writing is coming along. Unfortunately, many people don't get the memo and throw the question about carelessly, oblivious to the invisible sharp spikes in it that always prick a PhD student's delicate flesh.

I got answers to some of my questions as I progressed through my journey. I also became gradually confident in my abilities, and I was able to challenge myself to move outside my comfort zone. Although self-doubt never melted completely and occasional insecurities arose, they did not stop me from actively chasing my big dreams.

If you are unsure whether to pursue a PhD, this book is for you. In it, you will gain some insights from those who intentionally postponed starting their PhDs. If you are a prospective student applying for a PhD program, you will learn some strategies and hear some advice for securing scholarships and choosing the right university, research topic, and PhD advisor. If you are an ongoing PhD student, this book will give you tips and tricks on how to thrive and excel in your doctoral journey. You will learn some strategies for dealing with occasional paralyzing mental blocks, discover how to work efficiently, and familiarize yourself with some dos and don'ts of the PhD journey. Since success always leaves clues, you will also learn from the valuable experiences of some predecessors so you won't have to reinvent the wheel and can, hopefully, channel your energies and valuable time into your research.

Although our journeys are bound to be different, they will have plenty of common themes and lessons we can teach each other. It is my deepest hope that this book's strategies, pieces of advice, and tips and tricks for enrolling and thriving in a PhD program offer insight into your journey. When I was stuck and doubting myself, I constantly sought out stories and experiences of students who had travelled a similar path. I didn't find many such stories. So, I promised one day to share my experiences so others did not have to struggle to get answers to some of the questions I struggled with. We are all diverse, with different beliefs, upbringings, and dreams. We should all share our stories, as often as possible, through whichever medium we can. That way, those who come after us will have diverse stories to read and learn from.

This book touches on key topics inherent to every PhD student's journey. They include:

- Whether to embark on earning a PhD
- How to fund your PhD

- Choosing a university, an advisor, and a research topic
- Some tips for the journey; e.g., how to prepare for your PhD viva voce (dissertation defence)
- Advice from predecessors

Kindly note that my thoughts, viewpoints, and pieces of advice are mostly informed by my personal experiences reading for DPhil in Engineering Science at the University of Oxford and transitioning from a Kenyan institution to an elite institution in the UK. The thoughts and advice from other contributors (mostly friends from my network) are clearly stated. You can find their biographies in the Contributor Biographies section at the end of this book. The main caveat is I can't provide all the answers to the PhD questions you might have or that might arise during your journey. And some strategies that were helpful to me might not apply in your case. But I've written about my experiences as honestly as possible, and hopefully, you will learn from and be encouraged by the stories and thoughts I share. A PhD journey is a personal experience, unique to everyone; one cannot blindly copy and paste another person's journey. Just because something didn't work for me does not mean it won't work for you. We can learn from and find comfort in each other's experiences and stories.

ONE
PhD Now, Later, or Never

What is a PhD? PhD is an abbreviation for Doctor of Philosophy, an English translation of the Latin name *Philosophiae Doctor* or *Doctor Philosophiae*. Other abbreviations commonly used are Ph.D. and DPhil. PhD is the most common degree at the highest academic level awarded following an extended period of research. Depending on the field of study, university, and whether the program is taken full-time or part-time, a PhD journey could span a period of two to ten years. At the end of most PhD programs is a submission of a doctoral thesis or dissertation (detailing original research undertaken) and an oral examination—commonly referred to as a viva voce or dissertation defence.

While trying to find a reasonable answer to the question of whether to embark on the PhD journey, I thought of this interesting conversation between the Cheshire Cat and Alice in the novel *Alice in Wonderland*.

'Would you tell me, please, which way I ought to go from here?'

'That depends a good deal on where you want to get to', said the Cat.

'I don't much care where—' said Alice.

'Then it doesn't matter which way you go', said the Cat.

Whether or not to embark on the PhD journey will largely depend on where you want to get to in your career. For me, embarking on a PhD journey wasn't on the list of things to try before my twenty-fifth birthday. But towards the end of my undergrad pursuing BSc in Mechanical Engineering at Jomo Kenyatta University of Agriculture and Technology, JKUAT in Kenya, I had developed a very strong passion for the branch of mechanical engineering called thermofluids. And I was sure I wanted to pursue a master's degree and maybe get a job afterwards. I was trying to follow in the footsteps of some engineers whom I greatly admired. I knew a master's degree was going to open more career doors and perhaps allow me to start my career at a higher income.

In my final undergrad year, with one semester to go, and overflowing with ambition, I applied for the Rhodes Scholarship. It was the most ambitious scholarship application I had ever submitted. Luckily, I made it through the rigorous selection process. After winning the scholarship in 2015, as I described in my first book, *The Bold Dream: Transcending the Impossible*, a classmate let me know it was possible to embark on a PhD directly after my BSc and skip earning a master's degree. It was then that the bold seed of embarking on a PhD journey was firmly planted deep in my heart and mind. The seed germinated and grew stronger over time, withstanding the scorching pressure from fear. I was going to transition from a relatively small university in Kenya to one of the best universities in the world (the Rhodes Scholarship is only taken at the University of Oxford). To say the impending transition was scary is an understatement. After weeks of extensive consultation and preparation, I was ready to give the PhD route a go. Through the University of Oxford's website, I identified and contacted a professor who worked on thermofluids projects. He later agreed to be my PhD supervisor. We will talk more about PhD advisors later.

Although I was psychologically prepared for a postgraduate degree, I wasn't prepared for the PhD journey. I had to learn to adapt fast. My PhD journey, especially during the first years, would have been much easier had I talked to some ongoing PhD students, read some books to gain rough insights on the journey, and understood what it takes to earn a PhD at an elite institution. If I were to go back in time, would I choose a PhD route? Absolutely. But I would take some time, in the beginning, to prepare psychologically. Aside from invaluable skills like courage to try new things and the grit that the PhD journey has ingrained in me, earning a PhD has also opened more diverse career doors for me. For instance, without a PhD, I wouldn't have qualified for the Schmidt Science Fellowship—a postdoctoral fellowship that has honed my multidisciplinary research skills and leadership skills and, hence, better prepared me for careers in academia and industry.

Why pursue a PhD? Here are some reasons different people pursue one.

- Love of research, love of discovery, and wanting to become an expert in a particular field
- The satisfaction of climbing the academic ladder
- Access to more career options
- As a prerequisite to becoming a university professor

- For status and prestige
- Higher future earning potential
- Fulfilling a personal and/or family dream
- To develop transferable skills, like grit and problem-solving

In *The 7 Habits of Highly Effective People*, Stephen Covey talks about the carpenter's rule: "measure twice, cut once.... You have to make sure that the blueprint, the first creation, is really what you want, that you've thought everything through. Then you put it into bricks and mortar.... You begin with the end in mind".[1] Before embarking on your PhD journey, try as much as possible to think ahead and ask yourself if a PhD is necessary for your future career and plans. This journey, a seemingly endless and tumultuous one, will demand a lot of your resources; therefore, it's important to think about your destination before embarking on the journey. You may not predict your future career perfectly well. And your future career aspirations and many other things can, of course, be expected to change, and that is okay. But take the time to decide whether a PhD is a degree you must have and whether to embark on the journey now, forego it, or postpone it.

In *How to Survive Your PhD*, Dr Jason R. Karp gives this helpful advice on why you must take time to decide whether to embark on the PhD journey.

> Because of its long-term nature, you had better find out what you're getting yourself into first and assess whether or not you can make the kind of commitment required for a doctoral program.... If you pursue your PhD when you're still young and in school, you may lag behind your college friends in job experience and life stability for up to ten years as you graduate. Think about this for a moment. Now ask yourself, "Do I still want to pursue a PhD? Whether you're married or have children are also important considerations, especially because you don't want to sacrifice the time you could otherwise spend

with your family…something will always be sacrificed and perhaps neglected as you pursue your degree.[2]

As you decide whether to embark on a PhD, the thoughts and advice summarised in Table 1.1 from some of my friends may be insightful. You can find my friends' biographies in the Contributor Biographies section at the end of this book.

Table 1.1: Some reasons for postponing a PhD

Why did you postpone your PhD?

Mercy Akoth

While I could pursue my PhD under the Rhodes Scholarship, I opted not to for the following reasons:

1. Professional/Career Goals. At the time I won the Rhodes Scholarship, I was working towards my UK's Institute and Faculty of Actuaries, IFoA actuarial qualification. My short- to medium-term goal was to practice as an actuary; the actuarial qualifying exams, and not necessarily a PhD, would enable me to realise this goal. I, therefore, felt that the Oxford 1+1 MBA would better suit my career goals—allowing me to major and advance my knowledge in Statistics in year one and sharpen and advance my business acumen and strategic thinking in year two.

2. Lack of a suitable PhD program. I could have pursued my actuarial exams alongside a PhD. Hence, pursuing a PhD should still have been an option. But the lack of a suitable PhD program/supervisor to suit my actuarial background left me with fewer choices.

3. Family. At the time I won the Rhodes Scholarship, I was dating. My then-boyfriend (he is now my husband) and I had the intention of settling down sooner rather than later. Taking up the scholarship meant we had to reconsider our plans, and we felt that a two-year stint at Oxford worked best for us, rather than three or four years if I had gone the PhD route. However, we later learnt that we could have explored coming to Oxford with him as my spouse; hence, we probably shouldn't have worried about the long time apart if I had done a PhD. We have since both qualified as actuaries and are pursuing our careers in the London market. We intend to register for a part-time PhD at some point since we both aspire to teach at a university in the long term, after gaining industry experience to make our in-class delivery more powerful.

Anonymous Student

I am taking a 1-2-year break from school to gain **professional experience** and develop a PhD project before starting the journey. I pursued both of my graduate studies without having extensive professional experience. So, I'm taking 1-2 years to gain experience and also apply the theory I've gained so far by engaging in person with forced migrants. (My training is in forced migration and refugee studies.) I am equally using this opportunity to design a probable PhD project. I want to be more intentional with what I end up doing and have a passion for whatever PhD project I shall be pursuing. I must mention, though, that during my first master's, I received a PhD offer. Despite my excitement, the news filled me with loads of anxiety. I felt unprepared to go into a PhD program. I wasn't quite confident with my academic writing skills or critical analysis of literature skills that would be required to undertake a heavily independent 3-4 years of study like most PhDs at the University of Oxford do. Long story short, I instead pursued a second master's degree to hone the very skills I felt inadequate in. I know one can never be 100 percent ready, but were I to proceed to a doctorate now, as compared to then, I'd be better prepared and could effectively make the most of my time there.

Rono Kipkorir

Two main reasons have greatly influenced me to postpone my PhD studies: the need for a **break** and **family**. I've spent the last three years studying for my master's degree in a foreign country. The studies have been rigorous, and the project I was working on took a toll on me. After my master's studies, I felt I deserved a break from the rigours of academic study and research. I also remember forcing myself to have an academic break after my five-year bachelor's studies. I only started my master's studies three years after undergrad. So, taking an academic break is nothing new to me. It gives me time to recharge my mind and body, take stock of what I've learnt, and refocus my ambitions. Moreover, I have a young family. I moved in with my fiancée about two years ago and my first-born daughter was born in May 2020. She was born while I was completing my master's studies abroad. I only got to meet her four months after she was born. So, I was understandably excited to finally be near her. If I had elected to pursue my PhD so soon after returning home, I would have again had to be separated from my young family and not been around to spend quality time with my daughter and her mother. I knew I had the responsibility to be near them and to be a father-figure to my daughter, watching her grow through her formative years. Since I'm not planning to do my PhD studies locally, I hope my daughter will soon grow up to understand why I have to be away again. Then, I will be ready to start my PhD studies.

Godfrey Momanyi

I am taking the time to decide whether to do a PhD abroad or in Kenya. This depends on the performance of **my company** (Energy Intelligence Africa) in the next two years. If I'm progressing well in Kenya, then I will proceed to enrol for a PhD locally. The main reason I plan to enrol for a PhD is to enable me to access more opportunities in the research market.

Patrick Kiprotich Korir

In the final year of my master's studies, I was open to both pursuing a PhD and working in the industry. However, I was more interested in **working in the industry** because I wanted to put the knowledge, gained from so many years of studies, into practice. I thought it was more fulfilling in the industry since you can see things transform rapidly from an idea to a product in a customer's hands. Venturing into a PhD would mean more dedicated time in the laboratory with less actualization of the work, at least instantaneously. It's worth mentioning that there are industrial PhDs where one is fully based in the industry and the work translates to tangible products or being adopted by a company. This would be more fun, in my opinion. All said and done, I did not cast away the PhD thought completely, but I chose to postpone it to a later time.

TWO
Funding Your PhD

Once you have decided to embark on the PhD path, funding your PhD will be one of the key factors to consider. The PhD program will not only take up lots of time, but also take a toll on your finances. Whether you are self-financing (including taking out loans that you'll have to repay later) or receiving scholarships, a lot of thought needs to go into the cost/benefit analysis, unless of course you have loads of money and depleting your reserves while financing your PhD isn't on your list of worries. The total cost of your PhD will obviously depend on so many factors, including the institution where you enrol in your PhD program, the field of research, the length of your PhD, etc. For instance, during the 2022-2023 University of Oxford's academic year, a PhD program at the Department of Engineering Science costs about £29,000 per year (for a foreign student), totalling up to more than £110,000 if the program takes four years. And note that this estimated amount didn't factor in living expenses, which can be quite high in expensive cities like Oxford, UK.[3]

I was very lucky to secure the Rhodes Scholarship because it funded all my PhD. The scholarship fully covered all the major expenses, including the university application fee, living stipend, settling-in allowance, health insurance, and economy class flight tickets—one from Nairobi to London (at the start of the course) and another from London to Nairobi (at the end of the course). Securing the scholarship saved me a great deal of financial stress. I can't imagine how much more stressful my PhD journey would have been if I'd had to worry about finances.

I learned about the Rhodes Scholarship in my final year of my undergrad through a classmate who kept close tabs on postgraduate scholarships. One day, as we sat idly awaiting a lecturer, he came to my desk and wrote a website address (scholars4dev.com) on the back of my exercise book. He told me to check out an interesting scholarship listed on that website called the Rhodes Scholarship. I was restless the rest of that class. I couldn't wait for the lecture to end so I could check the website. After the class, I hurriedly made my way to the university pavilion (the only place with reliable internet connectivity on campus) to check out the scholarship. I had never heard of the Rhodes Scholarship before. Once I visited the website, it didn't take me long to realise the scholarship was quite prestigious. What dimmed my excitement, though, was that the scholarship is only taken at the University of Oxford. Even if I secured the scholarship, did I have good enough grades to secure admission at the University of Oxford? I didn't think I had a chance.

After weeks of relentless pressure from my classmate to give it a try, I buckled. After all, what did I have to lose? Nothing. The journey of applying for the Rhodes Scholarship began. I collected all the required documentation, obtained letters of reference, and casually submitted my application. The hardest part of the application process was preparing the personal statement—an essay that answers questions like: Who are you? What matters to you? What are your aspirations/dreams? I could convincingly talk about my achievements and make a case for why I was the best candidate for the scholarship. However, I struggled when it came to putting that same story down on a piece of paper. Most of my application time was spent preparing the statement. I combed the internet, reading countless publicly available personal statements. Then I spent several weeks drafting, editing, and proofreading the statement till I got a reasonable final product that I used for the application. Looking back now, I think the following top three strategies helped me prepare a good personal statement.

- **The more specific you are the better.** For example, instead of just writing 'I was a recipient of an undergraduate scholarship', give more details and be more specific: How many applicants did the undergraduate scholarship attract that year? How many interview stages did you go through? How many students were awarded the scholarship in the end? You could write something like this: 'I was a recipient of the James Finlay Trust Scholarship, a competitive annual scholarship awarded to only two students (selected from more than 1500 applicants through a series of four rigorous interview stages).' Writing about your recognitions and achievements this way gives the assessors a clear idea of how competitive the award/recognition was so they can correctly contextualise your amazing capabilities and achievements. This applies to everything else: If writing about a leadership position you held, give such details as how long you

had the position and what were some of the key achieve-
ments/highlights from your tenure. If writing about extra-
curricular activities that you took part in, give more details;
e.g., I competed in two editions of the East Africa University
Games. I played in the first eleven of my university women's
soccer team, which won both editions). If writing about an
organisation/volunteering/community club you founded,
give details about how big the organisation is. Include some
of the key achievements/impacts it has had thus far. Have
you garnered any notable funding/partnership?

- **Make it unique to you.** You can consult all you want, and
read all the examples from the internet, but in the end, you
must make your statement uniquely yours. If someone read
it and met you, they should unmistakably know you are the
same person. There is a reason why the word 'personal' is in
the name of this type of statement. The personal statement
gives you a chance to answer some key questions: Who are
you? How did you get here? What have been some of the
challenges and opportunities on your journey thus far? What
wakes you up in the morning? What are your dreams and
aspirations? How will this scholarship help steer you in the
direction of your dreams?

- **Start drafting the statement as early as possible.** This way,
you will have a chance to draft and refine, ensuring that
all the key points have been captured. You have so many
exciting stories that need to be unpacked, repackaged, and
handpicked to fit a common set thread. This process applies
even more if there is a word limit for your essay. Compressing
your whole life and your amazing accomplishments into, say,
a thousand words isn't a mean feat. You need ample time to
draft, refine, and trim it to the required word/page count.
In many instances, your scholarship might provide you with
a bounded prompt—a guide that reads something like, 'In

not more than 1000 words, address your general interests and activities. What inspires you? What are your passions? Discuss your aims and priorities and the contributions you have made and hope to make to the world and/or communities of which you are part.' In such a case, make sure your statement addresses all the specific topics, themes, and issues spelled out in the prompt.

After clicking the submit button, I sort of forgot all about the Rhodes Scholarship. And since I believed I had the slimmest chance of being shortlisted, I kept applying for other scholarships I thought I had a higher chance of winning. Then one fine afternoon in late October 2014, an email that forever altered the course of my life hit my mailbox. The email was from the National Secretary for the Rhodes Trust in Kenya. The subject and the body of the email didn't give away much information, so I just skimmed through it and rushed to open the attachment. In the first paragraph, I spotted the phrase 'I am pleased to confirm...' and knew I had been shortlisted. The first paragraph read:

Dear Gladys,

In connection with your application for the award of the Rhodes Scholarship, I am pleased to confirm that you are one of the candidates shortlisted by the Selection Committee. Your interview will be held at the Southern Sun Hotel, Nairobi on Thursday 6th November 2014 at 11.40 a.m....

I later learned that only five of us had been shortlisted. Only two students would be awarded the scholarship. On 7 November 2014, I was informed that I (and one other student) had been selected as Rhodes Scholars, and we would join the class of 2015. It was my best news for that year. In the days that followed, I wondered what the selection committee had seen in me. From my perspective, I hadn't achieved as much as the other finalists.

Years later, while narrating my interview experience, a friend noted something I found interesting. Sometimes one might not have the best of qualifications or achievements, but they still win the scholarship. Why? Maybe the selection committee contextualised their situation. They carefully analysed the applicant's trajectory, and they could foresee a huge promise and potential in the applicant's future if they were given a chance. So never undermine yourself, your journey, or your dreams. Whatever your story is, confidently put your best foot forward. Tell your unique story; share your accomplishments and dreams with conviction, and leave the rest to the selection committee.

Based on my experience applying and securing a scholarship, I found these top three tips to be very helpful.

- **Get quality references.** It's sad to go through the hectic scholarship application process, pouring all your energy and time into perfecting your essays, only for your references to spoil a chance of winning the scholarship for you. Choose references you absolutely know won't let you down. References who can speak well and provide meaningful details about you. Simple things like sharing your resume (or a draft of your statements) with them will go a long way in ensuring that they fine-tune their reference to reflect who you are as presented in your resume/personal statement. Also, don't forget to remind your references to complete and submit their recommendations on time.

- **Be authentic.** Just like I noted in writing your personal statement, be authentic during the interview. The selection committee, when they interact with you during the interview, should see a mirror of the person on the personal statement. You may want to talk to some alumni of the scholarship as well as other people you think might offer useful insights and pieces of advice to help you prepare and have an idea of what to expect, but during your interview, present your authentic self. You may be denying yourself a chance by trying to be a photocopy of someone else.

- **Don't underplay your achievements**. One panellist was extremely impressed that I had successfully juggled my studies, leadership roles, playing soccer, and participating in track and field events. But since I had done all these extra-curricular activities almost all my life, they had stopped being anything special to me. So, when I was asked about extracurricular activities I had done, I casually narrated that I had about seven track and field medals under my belt that I had earned during my undergrad. The panellist stopped me and asked that I restart the story, but with more confidence and pride. Never downplay your achievements. Write all about your achievements, awards, recognitions, and talents to the extent the word limit will allow. And don't forget to talk about them with confidence during your interview.

Every scholarship is unique and has varying eligibility criteria. Read extensively about the scholarship you are applying for so you can prepare adequately. Numerous bloggers and vloggers on the internet also write and talk about their scholarship application experiences. Check them out; you might get some strategies, tips, and tricks from them on how to make your application stand out.

If you are a prospective PhD student searching for scholarships, you might find these scholarship websites (that I collected from some of my friends) helpful.

- Find a PhD:
  https://www.findaphd.com
- Scholarships for Development:
  https://www.scholars4dev.com
- Opportunities for Africans:
  https://www.opportunitiesforafricans.com

- Academic Positions:
  https://academicpositions.com/find-jobs
- Scholarship Positions:
  https://scholarship-positions.com
- Study Portals Scholarships:
  https://www.scholarshipportal.com
- Opportunity Desk:
  https://opportunitydesk.org

I asked some of my friends to talk about their scholarships, including the name of the scholarship and how they learned about it. Their answers are summarized in Table 2.1.

Table 2.1: Some possible scholarship avenues

Scholarship Avenues

Orina Masaki

Rhodes Scholarship. I was made aware of the Rhodes Scholarship by a high school friend. I clearly recall the crisp winter morning when this friend, who was aware of my interests, asked me to consider applying for the Rhodes Scholarship. I was at that time on an exchange program at the University of Manitoba in Canada, spending the first few minutes of an early morning catching up with friends in Kenya before embarking on the day's work. From that moment, I researched the scholarship, and with the overwhelming support of mentors at my alma mater, the University of Nairobi, I put myself forward for it.

Priyanka Dhopade

University scholarship (awarded to anyone who applies for a PhD and meets the GPA requirements). My PhD supervisor guided me through the process once we agreed I was interested in doing a PhD on his offered project.

Miriam Jerotich Kilimo

Rhodes Scholarship. I got the Rhodes Scholarship for my master's studies at the University of Oxford. I learnt about the scholarship through the Scholarship Office at my undergraduate institution, Dartmouth College, USA. My PhD studies are funded fully by Emory University, which provides full tuition and stipends for doctoral students.

Suhas Mahesh

Rhodes Scholarship. I learnt about the scholarship through word of mouth.

Javier Stober

Internal Stanford University scholarship, plus teaching assistantships. I taught seventeen courses, most of which earned me full funding.

Alex Kirui

Most state universities in the US have funding from their respective states. Before you apply, first check if they have funding. Some private universities offer PhD funding too.

Cephas Samende

Rhodes Scholarship. I learnt about the scholarship through a friend.

Mercy Nyamewaa Asiedu

Most PhD programs in biomedical engineering in the United States are fully funded. However, I also received a two-year Pratt-Gardner Fellowship and a one-year Global Health Fellowship from my university, which increased my stipend and went towards research projects.

Ndjodi Ndeunyema

Rhodes Scholarship. I learnt about the scholarship through word of mouth. Networking helped me secure these.

Marion Ouma

1. National Research Funding (NRF) South Africa, through my advisor.

2. Next Generation Social Sciences in Africa (www.ssrc. org), through a colleague.

Xiangkun (Elvis) Cao

Cornell Graduate Research Assistantship/Cornell Teaching Research Assistantship. I also received the following fellowships during my PhD at Cornell University: Launchpad Startup Fellowship by the Blackstone LaunchPad & Techstars, Marla and Barry ILR '90 Beck Entrepreneurship Fellowship by Cornell University, BP Advancing Energy Scholarship by BP PLC, INK Fellowship by Ixoraa Knowledge Foundation, Local Pathways Fellowship by UN Sustainable Development Solutions Network–Youth. Before Cornell, I received a Graduate Excellence Fellowship from McGill University. Most recently, I received the German Chancellor Fellowship from the Humboldt Foundation. I came to know about the fellowships from word of mouth and by searching in multiple scholarship databases. I think my mixed background in translational research, policymaking, and entrepreneurship, and my expertise in multiple engineering disciplines has positioned me as a unique applicant for these fellowships.

THREE
Choosing a University, Advisor, and Research Topic

3.1 Which university is right for you?

You may decide to study in a university within your home country, or you may decide to study abroad. Sometimes external factors, such as family or funding, might limit your choices. For instance, in my case, my scholarship dictated that I undertake my PhD at the University of Oxford in the UK. It worked out all right for me. I didn't mind going abroad to study for my PhD since I had always desired to study abroad.

Take time to decide where, based on your particular circumstances, it is best to undertake your PhD. Start your search early. Consult your family members, friends, and trusted educational advisors. Some of the questions you may want to consider when choosing a PhD institution include:

- Does the university have an accredited program in your field?
- Do its standards and prestige meet your expectations?
- If you have a scholarship, does your scholarship limit your choice of a university?
- Do you want to study in a small college or a large university?
- Is the university located in your desired location and region?

Don't underestimate the impact that location will have on your general experience. If you can't handle nippy weather, you might want to reconsider studying at a university located in Greenland. Would you like to live in a major city or a small town? In her book *Hooded: A Black Girl's Guide to the Ph.D.*, Dr Malika Grayson notes how a university's location/surroundings can impact your mood and general mental health. Dr Grayson confesses that she regrets giving little thought to the location of her PhD university.

> I gave very little thought to the town I would be living in when I chose this school [Cornell University]. In hindsight, I should have. Simple things such as airport accessibility and flight cancellations due to inclement weather were common issues. They may seem like things that can be overlooked, but when you combine these with all the other "simple" setbacks, each one adds a layer of frustration to your overall experience.[4]

If you are planning to undertake your studies abroad, it's paramount to gather as much information as possible about what to expect and what to brace yourself for when you get to your university. Do your search by reading books, checking news about your university through the internet, and talking to other students. If you are a minority student, check whether the university you are about to enrol in has a department to support minority students; believe me, there is a high chance that you might need its services once in a while. If you are going to study at a university abroad, I recommend you educate yourself on some important issues like the local religion, culture, and weather so you know what to expect. Looking back, I didn't do a good job of researching my university environment.

While on this topic of studying abroad, we can't avoid talking about a crucial document: a visa. Carefully check the visa requirements of the country you are going to. Start preparation early. Prepare all the documents required to process the visa way in advance. It also helps to mentally plan and prepare for a worst-case scenario. What if, for some reason, your visa is refused? Do you know whom you can talk to? Can you appeal?

My first UK visa application was rejected. I can't fully describe to you the mental and financial stress I went through following that rejection. I remember exactly where I was when I checked my email—in the middle of a farewell party my family had organised for me. It was early September 2015, and I was set to travel to the UK later that month. I was checking my email on my phone for the gazillionth time that day. Just as the email opened, I saw one unread email with the heading "Visa4UK…". I didn't bother to read the entire heading. I immediately opened the email and was utterly dejected. I had expected the email would let me know whether my visa application had been approved. Instead, it asked me to go to the visa application centre in Nairobi to collect my decision. I hated the word "decision." I was dying to find out what the visa decision was.

Early the following day, I hurriedly left home and embarked on a six-hour journey to collect my decision from the visa centre in the Westlands area of Nairobi. I passed the security check and headed directly to the collection counter. As a polite gentleman went through his documents to locate my file, I held my breath. At this point, my anxiety was threatening to swallow me alive. It had to be a positive decision. I couldn't picture myself going through the whole visa application process; I was running out of time. Plus, I couldn't afford to finance a second visa application fee. There was a health surcharge of £150 for every year you would be in the UK. I was applying for a five-year visa, meaning a total of £750 for health surcharge fees. Then there was the application fee, which was about £350. That brought the total visa cost to more than £1000. That was a whopping Ksh.150,000—a gigantic expense for a common *mwananchi* (ordinary person) like me.

"There you go". After what seemed like a decade, the gentleman had finally located my file. He handed me the file and went back to serving others in the queue. The 'decision' was lying enigmatically inside a white A4 envelope.* I couldn't wait any longer; curiosity was eating me alive. Outside the centre, I leaned on the staircase rail, unceremoniously tore the envelope, held my breath, and allowed the letter bearing the 'decision' to emerge slowly from the envelope. The title caused my stomach to churn as my eyes came in belligerent contact with the bold capital-letter-headed title of the two-page decision letter. "REFUSAL OF ENTRY CLEARANCE". One warm spherical tear fell on the paper as I tried so hard to fight back my tears lest I attract unwanted attention from the applicants streaming like ants in and out of the application centre. Reading further, I understood why my visa was declined; '...you were requested to produce a certificate issued by an approved clinic showing that you are free from infectious tuberculosis. You have not produced such a certificate. I, therefore, refuse your application.' The sentence bounced in my mind while I tried to make sense of its implication.

---

* A4 is the international standard paper size, which measures 8¼ x 11¾ in, or 210 x 297 mm. It is close to the equivalent US standard paper size of 8½ x 11.

Later, I sadly realised the list of required documents I had read was from some random website, not from the UK Home Office website. I was inexperienced with the whole issue of visa applications. In retrospect, I should have done extensive consultation to countercheck if I had all the documents needed before submitting my application. Perhaps I should have contacted my university's Student Immigration and Student Information department to confirm I had all the required documents needed for the visa application.

Pay fastidious attention to the issue of visas and religiously follow all the steps required during the application process to avoid unnecessary delays, expenses, and stresses. Also note that, depending on your level of English proficiency and country of residency, you may be required to provide an English test result. The good news is you can apply for the language test requirement to be waived; for instance, if you have studied for a university-level degree for at least four years in the English language. The bad news is the waiver application is not always successful, like in my case. My English language test requirement waiver was rejected, and I had to take the test. My program accepted either the International English Language Testing System, IELTS (with at least an overall score of 7.5 and at least a score of 7.0 in listening, reading, writing, and speaking components) or the Internet-based Test of English as a Foreign Language, TOEFL (with at least a score of 25 in listening, reading, writing, and speaking components). It took me about three months to prepare sufficiently for the test. Be sure to plan your time accordingly to prepare adequately, take the test, and get the results in time.

3.2 Choosing your PhD advisor

How do you choose your advisor? There are different ways to connect with a potential advisor. How you identify and get matched with an advisor could depend on many factors, including the practices and policies of your department or university. In *Hooded*, Dr Malika Grayson lists some of the questions (see below) that helped her settle on an advisor who was right for her. Perhaps you can learn from these questions too.

- What is their background, and how does it complement mine and my goals?
- Does this individual have the time and bandwidth to be invested in me?
- What makes them an effective advisor (are they respected?), and what is the feedback from other students?
- Does this person have the qualities and characteristics I look for and admire in a mentor?
- Will I be able to gain knowledge, professional growth, and opportunities under this person's tutelage?
- What relationship do they have with the diversity office or point of contacts at the school?[5]

In my case, after securing the scholarship, I began the process of identifying a potential advisor. I was certain I wanted to undertake a research project at the Department of Engineering Science. I was, however, torn between projects in Energy Systems and Storage, Tidal Energy, and Thermofluids. I ended up contacting several professors in all these fields. After some back and forth via emails and Skype calls, I made up my mind and settled for my first love—Thermofluids and Turbomachinery. In the third year of my undergrad, I had topped my class in the Engineering Thermodynamics course unit and won the Engineer Kariuki Thermodynamics Award. Engineer Kariuki was one of the senior lecturers at the university and a thermodynamics lecturer who started the award to inspire students to enter the thermofluids field. The award did its magic because it inspired me to study thermofluids.

I struggled quite a bit in contacting potential advisors. I would wonder why many of the professors I contacted never replied to my emails. When I look back now, I cringe and laugh at how poorly written and unprofessional those emails were. Perhaps that is why my emails didn't arouse the interest of ever-busy professors. When contacting potential advisors, it helps to place yourself in their shoes. If you were them, would you pay attention to that email? Is it succinct and professionally done? Remember, they are busy people with plenty on their plate. Be succinct and professional in your emails. Introduce yourself and state what you are hoping to get from them. If possible, attach a well-summarised and professional resume with relevant research information. Below is a version of an email (after many updates) I used to introduce myself to my potential advisors back in 2014. I didn't intern in the listed companies, but I have used them as an example of how to include relevant information for the role you are applying for. Your email doesn't have to be a replica of mine, but you will get the point from it. Also, if possible, consider using a professional email address like gladys.ngetich@gmail.com rather than one like gladeeez!!@gmail.com. How you package yourself matters a lot. If your email is poorly written, you might never get a reply. In his book *Deep Work: Rules for Focused Success in a Distracted World*, Cal Newport writes about a fascinating approach to emails that he noticed his professors applied:

> Their default behavior when receiving an e-mail message is to not respond...[as] they believed, it's the sender's responsibility to convince the receiver that a reply is worthwhile. If you didn't make a convincing case and sufficiently minimise the effort required by the professor to respond, you didn't get a response.[6]

Here is my email:

Subject: Joining Your Research Group as a PhD Student

Dear Professor XYZ,

My name is Gladys Ngetich, a final year student at Jomo Kenyatta University in Kenya pursuing a BSc in Mechanical Engineering. Based on my current GPA, I expect to graduate in July 2015 with First Class Honours of 4.0 GPA. I am writing to express my interest in joining your research group as a PhD student. I am available for a Skype call at your convenience.

I have secured a full scholarship from the Rhodes Trust to undertake doctoral research at the University of Oxford. I have an interest in the field of thermofluids and turbomachinery. I have undertaken internships at some of the top thermal energy companies in Kenya, including Thika Power Plant and Geothermal Development Company where I worked on thermofluids-related projects. For my final-year undergraduate design project, I worked on a thermofluids thesis titled: Optimisation of a Novel Hydraulic Propeller Turbine Using CFD. The thermofluids-related course units, internships, and class projects I have undertaken have given me a broader perspective, knowledge, and skills in the field of thermofluids.

Find attached my CV, transcripts, and my recent publications.

Thank you in advance for your time and consideration. I look forward to hearing from you.

Regards,
Gladys Ngetich
Rhodes Scholar-Elect 2015, Kenya

This professional way of contacting people does not stop with advisors. While gathering information about your potential lab, university, or advisor, you may want to talk with some current students as well as alumni. When contacting them through whichever medium—be it Email, LinkedIn, Facebook, Twitter, etc.—be professional. Introduce yourself and make it clear what information you would like to gather from them. This professionalism will not only increase the chance that they will get back to you, but they will then be able to offer helpful responses.

The PhD journey can be quite an isolating and lonely one. Perhaps the best thing that can happen to a PhD student is finding an advisor who will unfailingly have your back and help you stand on your feet. Someone who will make it their business to help you thrive and grow in your research. Someone who will be invested not only in your PhD journey but also in you as a whole, rounded individual. You need an advisor who will regard you as a complex human being who doesn't exist in one dimension, but is a multidimensional individual with dreams, hopes, aspirations, fears, family, and a life outside of the lab.

At the onset, it may be difficult to know your potential advisor's personality or whether they will be supportive and invested in your journey. This becomes even more challenging if you're planning to undertake your PhD studies abroad at a university whose environment and faculty members you barely know. This is where you do your homework. Gather as much information as possible from current students and alumni from your potential department. While you gather information from people, always bear in mind that experiences are sometimes unique to an individual. If they had a horrible experience, it doesn't necessarily mean you will too. So, advance with caution. But if 100 percent of the students who went through the hands of that potential advisor had a horrible experience, then maybe it's wise to play safe and reconsider your choice of advisor.

I was extremely lucky to find an advisor who supported me throughout my PhD journey. Retrospectively, my journey would have been horrendous were it not for him. Without a master's degree, I joined the lab with barely any research experience. I had to learn almost all research-related skills—reference management, literature review, scientific writing, etc.—from scratch. He patiently guided me through every step along the way. One of my best memories was when he taught me the simple technique of using an Excel sheet to collect and record literature review information. From that day, the normally dull process of literature reviewing instantly transformed into something more exciting. You will read more about this situation and find a picture of the Excel sheet later in this book in Table 4.3.1. Even outside research, my advisor would often keep a mental record of my 400-meter hurdles (my Varsity track and field specialty) performance as well as the personal best times I was aiming for. His constant support within, and without, the lab gave me an immense boost and morale that trickled down to my research.

In dealing with your advisor, it helps to keep in mind that they are human and, just like everyone else, have emotions. They go through high and low moments. They are also grappling with deadlines. And they aren't immune to fear and insecurities. Even though it's your right as a student to be properly supervised by your advisor, and hopefully, no one forced them to supervise you, still, being considerate will go a long way. This also applies to your committee members (if you have them). In everything you do, from writing them an email requesting people to be on your committee to sending them your manuscripts, always remember that they are human beings. Dr Karp, in writing about 'Choosing Your Committee', gives an insightful piece of advice:

> When you finally have the right committee assembled, seek and utilise the advice of its members…. Tell them

how you value their opinions...while you don't have to brown nose or gush compliments on every occasion, your committee members are people first, with similar tendencies as other people. The more they like you, the more likely they will vote in your favour when it's time for your qualifying exams and dissertation defense.[7]

If an opportunity presents itself, and you can spare some time out of the ever-busy PhD schedule, nominate your advisor for Inspirational Advisor, or similar awards or recognitions. This goes without saying, but only nominate them for such recognitions if you strongly believe they deserve it. I once nominated my advisor for the annual Rhodes Scholarship Inspirational Educator Award. The award is made annually by the Rhodes Trust to recognise and celebrate exceptional educators/mentors who go above and beyond to help their students realise their potential. I am certain my advisor put extra effort into mentoring me so I could be on par with my colleagues. And for that, I was beyond thankful, which is why I nominated him. You can read more about why I consider my advisor one of the people who have been crucial in my academic journey in my co-authored book, *The Bold Dream*. My advisor was proud of the award and conspicuously displayed it in his office.

3.3 Choosing a PhD research topic

How do you settle on a doctoral research topic? A ton of strategies exist. Dr Malika Grayson recommends:

> Find something that fuels your fascination more than it sparks frustration.... If you find yourself more frustrated than fascinated over time, then it may be time to rethink your research.... Frustration will happen, but it should be well-balanced with your yearning to move the needle in the subject area further.[8]

In his *New York Times* article "Four Steps to Choosing a College Major," Nathan Gebhard gives the following advice on choosing your major. These tips might also help you when choosing your research topic.

- Forget passion; follow an interest. Sometimes we get paralysed trying to figure out what our passion is. If you are struggling to find your passion, try instead to find an interest and nurture it, knowing that passion is a process and not an end goal.
- Separate your goals from other people's goals for you. Make sure you are pursuing a topic that you want to pursue, not what your family, teachers and friends wish for you.
- Put your decisions in a real-world context. Do your expectations closely match real-world reality?
- Be flexible. Even with real-world expectations in mind, you'll encounter uncomfortable sharp bends. Proceed with a flexible mindset; always be ready and willing to redesign your interests to go with the flow.[9]

I asked some of my friends how they settled on their PhD research topic and their PhD institution. See Table 3.1 for a summary of their responses.

Table 3.1: How did you settle on your PhD research topic and university?

How did you settle on your PhD research topic and university?
Orina Masaki
<u>PhD Topic</u> I got onto my PhD project at a moment of failure. I was completing a master's in neuroscience at the University of Oxford, working on a project that was to transform into my PhD work. It was clear that I was struggling with this project. While I can look back now and confidently say

that I was never suited for that work (the project involved recording electrical activities from neurons in a petri dish), at that time, I had interpreted the failure as not working hard enough. It was also the first meaningful failure of my academic journey.

At the end of the master's, I gave up the summer break that was before the PhD started to make progress on the project. I had hoped that reaching the 10,000-hour mark would mean mastery and success. This did not work. Just before the official start date for the PhD, I approached the neuroscience graduate studies leadership to let them know I was not going forward with the project or PhD. To my surprise, the leadership team suggested I keep my PhD student status, while exploring opportunities in different labs. A biologist may want to refer to this as being an uncommitted stem cell—with all possibilities ahead, including that of not pursuing a PhD. Further, I do not recall the leadership team specifying a time frame for this.

I sat down in my room, took out a pen and paper, and started jotting down topics that I had been keen on during the coursework for the master's program. This led me to a series of lectures that had been delivered by two researchers from the Department of Psychiatry, on 'how antidepressants work in the brain.' I had been fascinated by this subject, and without specific academic requirements, had read quite extensively on it. I reached out separately to the two researchers, only to find out that they collaborated for the most part in their work. I was struck by their kindness. With that, and only about a week after dropping my original PhD research plan, I had a new academic home. I was back onto the PhD track. I would go on to investigate the biological mechanisms of depression, including carrying out some of the initial studies on a potential novel antidepressant medication. I would be the first from my master's cohort to successfully defend a PhD thesis.

PhD Institution: University of Oxford, UK

The choice of my PhD institution was majorly dictated by my scholarship: the Rhodes Scholarship, which can only be taken at the University of Oxford.

Priyanka Dhopade

PhD Topic

I knew I wanted to do something related to fluid dynamics and preferably related to aeroplanes. I came across a project listed by a professor at UNSW Canberra that was fully funded, meaning he had already secured the funding for a student's stipend from the government, so my stipend would be guaranteed for at least three years, which I assumed was the full duration of a PhD. The topic was also well-defined and scoped, meaning it was something specific I could do research on. This held a bigger appeal to me than defining the topic myself. I just didn't have the confidence or knowledge to do that, but that may be different for you.

PhD Institution: UNSW Canberra, Australia

I had just finished my Master of Engineering at Monash University in Australia and wanted to continue with my studies through a PhD. I looked around for PhD projects that were advertised at Monash, and elsewhere in Australia. Rather than focus on the university, I wanted to find a topic that would be suitable and interesting to work on. I was googling a lot and came across many professors' profiles on their university web pages listing their research areas and available projects.

Miriam Jerotich Kilimo

PhD Topic

As I went through my undergraduate education, I became very interested in issues of identity and belonging in a community or country. For example, I was interested in why some communities choose to circumcise their girls as part of marking their identity. I was also interested in why people like to ask each other about their ethnic identity, and the ways people shift between identifying themselves by their ethnic and their national identity. By the time I finished my undergraduate studies, I knew I wanted to pursue a PhD in anthropology to research more on the themes of identity and belonging.

During my master's, I researched legislation against female circumcision, which helped me focus more on identity and belonging in a nation and community. By the time I was ready to apply for my PhD, I was no longer interested in pursuing female circumcision as a research topic.

I chose my PhD topic because I was interested in the ways politicians in Kenya were debating how to fully implement the two-thirds gender principle, a gender quota for increasing women's political representation. I wanted to research the dynamics around the quota: why it kept failing to pass, and what that meant in terms of how people perceive women who are nominated into political office. Through researching the gender quota, I wanted to learn more about identity and belonging from the perspective of women's political representation. Research topics often come from the things that interest us the most. For me, researching identity and belonging almost feels like I am researching myself and learning the ways I can live in this world.

<u>PhD Institution: Emory University, USA</u>

I applied to more than ten PhD anthropology programs, which I don't recommend people do! In the end, I had to decide between four programs. I chose my particular program/university because of several factors—a generous funding package, hearing wonderful things about my potential advisor, and the existence of a warm supportive community of PhD students. I also liked that the school had an African Studies program where I felt I could find an intellectual community.

As I've progressed in the PhD program, I've come to value more the importance of having a good advisor. A good advisor plus a generous funding package are the two most important things I would advise potential students to prioritise. A good advisor will look out for opportunities for you beyond your PhD program and ensure that you are hitting the milestones you need to in the program. A generous funding package will ensure that you aren't worrying about how to pay your bills and can have some fun.

Suhas Mahesh

<u>PhD Topic</u>

A sequence of internships during my undergrad piqued my interest in semiconductor physics. So, the broad field I wanted to work in was clear. Beyond that, I made my decision mostly based on whether the culture of the research group would be a good fit. Culture includes supportive peers, a culture of rigour, sufficient research funding, and a supervisor who spends enough time with their students. I believe every topic is interesting if you dive into it deeply enough; therefore, the particular research problem wasn't important to me. In any case, I didn't have the broad knowledge of several fields required to make a proper assessment.

PhD Institution: University of Oxford, UK

My choice had to be Oxford because I accepted the Rhodes Scholarship (which is only taken at the University of Oxford). While things worked out for me, if I had to do it again, I would set aside the university's brand name and scrutinise research groups instead. All top universities typically provide similar resources. It's really the culture of the group that is the make-or-break factor. I spoke to half-a-dozen current and past members of my PhD group before making my choice.

Javier Stober

PhD Topic

Based on passions and success in courses leading to that topic.

PhD Institution: Stanford University, USA

I made my choice based on the quality of the program and the culture.

Alex Kirui

PhD Topic

In my case, and as is the case for most chemistry PhDs in the US, you don't choose your research topic until your second semester in residence. That leaves you with a whole first semester to understand research areas in your department and also understand the faculty before you make your final choice.

In my case, I didn't know what research area/topic I would venture into when I started my first semester. I made my choice after talking to different faculty members and senior students. That came in November 2017 after I had already started my classes in August 2017. That isn't always the case, especially if you aren't a chemistry major. I've met people who had to choose their research topics before they reported to school.

Whatever the case, always visit your department's website and understand different research areas. If possible, try to email a few students or people in your area of study.

PhD Institution: Louisiana State University, USA

I got advice from my lecturers who were former students here. It's easy to get an admission where people from your country (Kenyans in this case) have been previously admitted and left a mark of success.

Another important factor is funding. I find it easier to get fully funded scholarships/assistantships in STEM (science, technology, engineering, and mathematics) fields compared to arts and humanities, but that does not rule out the possibility of getting a scholarship if you aren't a STEM major. Most scholarships in the US come as graduate research assistantships or graduate teaching assistantships.

Cephas Samende

PhD Topic

Firstly, with the help of my supervisor, I identified a project I was interested in from various research projects that were underway in the lab. Then, I studied the project in detail to gain an understanding of it and its objectives while noting gaps in the way the project was approached/designed and implemented and the intended results. Finally, with more than three gaps identified, I used a decision tree while consulting my supervisor and reviewing relevant literature to identify, rank, and choose three potential research topics. The first preference was to be the main research topic, and the others were backup research topics.

PhD Institution: University of Oxford, UK

I didn't choose the university myself. I was awarded the Rhodes Scholarship, which requires scholars to pursue postgraduate studies at the University of Oxford.

Mercy Nyamewaa Asiedu

PhD Topic

I was interested in combining biomedical engineering with global health. The lab I joined had an ongoing research project to develop accessible technologies for cervical cancer screening, which I was interested in. I found that incoming PhD students typically join projects the lab is working on and has funding for. Or they can start projects that the Principal Investigator (PI) of the lab is interested in, rather than PhD students starting their own research projects. That is why a good PI/lab fit is really important.

PhD Institution: Duke University, USA

It had one of the top biomedical engineering programs, and also had an awesome global health certificate option. There was a lab at Duke University that I was interested in specifically. The lab combined biomedical engineering and global health—two areas I was interested in.

Marion Ouma

PhD Topic

I chose my topic because of discontent I had experienced as a development worker. I had questions about the appropriateness of social policy choices under implementation in some developing countries—the discontent and questions led to my research topic.

PhD Institution: University of South Africa, South Africa

I did not choose the university. Rather, I was interested in doing my PhD with a particular professor, so I went to the university he was at.

Xiangkun (Elvis) Cao

Excerpted from Medium.com[10]

PhD Topic

In a chemistry class in a small-town middle school in Jiangsu Province, China, Xiangkun (Elvis) Cao learned that scientists were attempting to use sunlight to convert water into hydrogen and oxygen. The revelation launched him on a career path with an equally bright future.

"I thought if this problem could be solved, it would be tremendous", said Cao, a third-year doctoral student who is majoring in mechanical engineering and working in Professor David Erickson's lab. "People need oxygen to survive, and hydrogen can be used as a fuel. Imagine being able to use the sun to get fuel from water, which is everywhere on the planet. That idea was the spark".

PhD Institution: Cornell University, USA

Excerpted from Lindau Nobel Laureate Meetings.[11]

It was pretty simple. I chose Cornell University for its excellence in engineering disciplines, and Ezra Cornell's promise—"any person...any study" to students of the University.

To me, this promise also has a personal meaning. As a first-generation student, I understood that my journey was never alone and it's essential to be part of a support group or network with peers and mentors of similar backgrounds. Throughout my study at Cornell, I was amazed by the supportive and inclusive environment for minorities.

The questions I get asked the most by many prospective PhD students are, 'Must I have a research topic and research proposal ready before starting an application for a PhD program? How long should the PhD research proposal be?' The answers to these questions vary greatly depending on your university, field of study, and a wide range of other factors. In some cases, you might be required to have a well-thought-out research proposal when applying for admission. Whereas in other scenarios, that isn't the case.

Back in 2014, after securing a full scholarship, I remember struggling to develop a PhD proposal—one of the compulsory materials for my admission as a PhD student. I had no idea what a PhD research proposal looked like, let alone how to develop it. Therefore, when I corresponded with my advisor, from the beginning, I candidly informed him that I barely had any research skills, and as such, I wasn't well equipped to develop a PhD proposal. What aggravated my situation was that I didn't have any particular research topic in mind. I only knew I was interested in the area of mechanical engineering called thermofluids. My potential advisor was exceedingly understanding. He guided me through the key steps of drafting the proposal. He shared some of his past conference and journal research papers with me so I could gather ideas about the possible range of research topics his group was undertaking. Reading through the research papers gave me insight into the research tools and facilities available in his lab. Ideas collected from those research papers came in handy a few weeks later when I drafted my PhD proposal. After hours of drafting the proposal, and with immeasurable help from my potential advisor, the proposal was in a good shape.

I submitted the PhD proposal during the December application cycle. About three months later, on 20 March 2015, I received an email from the University of Oxford's Graduate Admission Office that brightened so many days that followed. I had been officially accepted by the University of Oxford's Department of Engineering Science to dine at their table with other DPhil students. My PhD journey was about to start, and my academic life was about to be transformed forever. Here is the beginning of the email I received:

Dear Miss Ngetich,

Application for admission as a graduate student to the University of Oxford
I am delighted to inform you that your application for admission to the University of Oxford as a graduate student has been successful. We would like to offer you a place to read for the Doctor of Philosophy (DPhil) in Engineering Science....

Looking back now, I laugh at how I put myself through copious amounts of unnecessary pressure and stress during the application period. I had thought of a PhD proposal as something incredibly complex. I pictured it as a gigantic document, fifty pages or longer. After extensive consultation with my potential advisor, we produced the PhD research proposal, which to my utter surprise was only one page long (on a piece of A4 paper)! The PhD proposal followed a similar structure to the one outlined in Table 3.2.

Table 3.2: A summary of key aspects of a PhD research proposal

Title	The title should be **persuasive**. It should give an insight into what your research will be about. It should neither be too long nor too short.
Introduction	Give a brief introduction to **why** anyone should care about this topic. Towards the end of the introduction, talk a bit about the state-of-art, i.e., does the solution already exist? This helps you to expose an existing **gap** that, hopefully, your research will address.
Methodology	**How** will you go about researching the topic you have proposed? This is the body of the proposal, so put a lot of your efforts here. Try addressing the question: **Which/What** research methods, equipment will you employ? It helps to briefly talk about some realistic results/ outcomes that you expect will emerge from your research.
Conclusion	Give a **summary** of the proposal emphasising what the gap is, how your research will attempt to fill that gap, the implications of your research, and some expected future work.

Additional Information	It may help to add a sentence or two at the end of your proposal indicating that you have identified and started consultations with a **potential advisor**. For instance, *'I have been in touch with Professor XYZ, at the Department of XYZ, who has kindly agreed to supervise my research. This consultation will continue as I prepare to begin my PhD in the summer of 2015.'*

As you settle on your university, research topic, and advisor, do your due diligence. You will be based in that university, working day and night on that research topic, with the support of that advisor for anywhere between two and ten years (hopefully not longer). To dodge unnecessary stresses, choose a supportive environment where you will thrive and excel. A caveat here is that you won't always make the right choice, even with months and years of dedicated research on your university, research topic, or advisor. Sometimes, just too many issues are outside of your control. In such cases, remember that whatever your current choice is, good or bad, it isn't a lifelong sentence. Nathan Gebhard rightfully notes that:

> Most people are unsure when they're starting out. Where they end up isn't a direct result of their major; it's the result of a meandering process. Their major— whether they stuck with it or applied it in new ways— was the start of channelling their interests, values and skills into work that made the struggles and hard work it took to get there worth it.[12]

While not easy, you will have a few chances to recalibrate your decisions as you go along in your PhD journey (and possibly post-PhD). This PhD journey is only a small dot in the grand scheme of things in your life, so do your due diligence, march forward confidently, and proudly draw that dot.

FOUR
Some Tips for the PhD Journey

4.1 Inspiration is perishable: quit perfectionism and just start

In their book *Rework*, Jason Fried and David H. Hansson give some insightful suggestions on how we can improve the way we work. Perhaps my biggest takeaway from the book is the three-word title of their conclusion: Inspiration is perishable. They suggest that once inspiration strikes and you make up your mind to take on the challenge at hand—be it to further your studies, to apply for a scholarship, to learn a new skill, or to start exercising—you must act fast before the inspiration to take on that challenge expires. Commit yourself and act fast to make it difficult to turn back later.

How do you commit yourself? By paying a deposit to the gym, by registering the company, by signing a deal with the book publisher, by disclosing your ambition to your close trusted friends so they keep you accountable. Psychologists call this process of committing yourself before the inspiration expires a commitment device. In *Atomic Habits*, James Clear writes:

> Commitment devices increase the odds that you'll do the right thing in the future by making bad habits difficult in the present.... If you are excited about the business you want to start, email an entrepreneur you respect and set up a consulting call. When the time comes to act, the only way to bail is to cancel the meeting, which requires effort and may cost money.[13]

I set my commitment device by announcing my ambitious thesis submission deadline to my advisor. It was mid-December of 2018, and I was about two months into my fourth year of my PhD studies, when I terrifyingly approached my advisor's office for an early morning meeting. He had an open-door policy, so you could walk into his office and converse if he was free. I sat across from him in his airy, well-organised, spacious office with a nice view of the Bulstake Stream, which connects to the River Thames. The combination of pin-drop silence in the lab, wintery weather outside, and a burbly stream created a very peaceful environment that, unfortunately, I couldn't enjoy because an infinite number of questions were racing through my mind. I was worried about how the meeting would end because I was about to drop a bomb.

'Yes, Gladys, how may I help you today?' he asked after our normal chit chat.

'I aim to submit my thesis at the end of June 2019.' There was pin-drop silence. A million questions were written all over his face. He took a heavy, deep breath and let the bomb settle. I had officially committed myself to something that, deep inside of me, I wasn't even sure was possible. The thesis submission date I was confidently proposing was only six months away. If what remained of my work was experimental and numerical data analysis and writeup, the ambitious proposal would have made more sense. But I hadn't even started a substantial section of my thesis, which I thought was needed to complete my PhD. And to further complicate the already uncertain situation, to complete that part of the work, I had to partner with an external company that fabricated test samples for me. That part of the work required not less than six months. So, you can understand the pin-drop silence after I dropped the bomb. It was practically impossible. But didn't Norman Vincent Peale advise us to shoot for the moon so that even if we miss, we'll land among the stars? That morning, I was intentionally shooting for the moon.

'Gladys, you understand that what you are proposing is a very ambitious deadline?' he asked, his eyes intensely focused on me.

I had developed a good rapport with my advisor, and I always knew he had my back. Therefore, I wasn't scared to be vulnerable with him about my work or to have difficult conversations like these.

'Yes, I know', I replied.

Further elaborations were not needed because we both knew there were some more work to be done. The night before, I had fully prepared and braced myself for this course-altering meeting. And so, I brought up a suggestion in the form of a question.

'Do you think I've done enough to earn a PhD?'

Of all the vulnerable questions I had ever asked from the start of my PhD, this was the most vulnerable of all. My supervisor took a brief moment to think of an appropriate answer. Every second he remained quiet felt like a decade.

'Yes, as a matter of fact, I do. I think you have done enough to earn a PhD', he began. 'But for a start, why don't you prepare a rough sketch of what you envision your thesis chapters will look like?'

I felt like jumping across his desk to hug him. That was the answer my ears were longing for. There was no need to take time to map out my thesis chapters because I had done my homework the night before. I had prepared a well-thought-out rough sketch of what I wanted my thesis chapters and subchapters to look like. I pulled out a nicely stapled PDF document and slid it across the table to him. He picked it up and checked it carefully, taking his time before he responded.

'I like the layout. But we will need to extend some of the chapters a little bit.'

He had a penchant for using the pronoun 'we'. And I absolutely loved it. Usually, that 'we' mostly meant 'you', but still, it sounded comfortingly collaborative. It reassured me that I wasn't alone in the journey, that he was with me every step of the way. In that instant, I didn't care about any work that needed to be redone, edited, or extended. My supervisor had officially given me the green light to proceed to the final stretch of my PhD journey, and that meant the world to me. If everything went according to plan—a PhD student will tell you things don't always go according to plan—I would be done with my PhD the following summer, in the next six months! It sounded unbelievable even in my mind. Thesis submission wasn't the end of my PhD journey; a viva voce would follow a few months after the submission, but I didn't care. In about six months, I planned to hit the biggest milestone in my PhD career: submitting the final draft of my thesis.

'I'm confident I will have the first draft of my thesis on your desk by the end of April 2019.' My commitment device was now fully set.

I couldn't concentrate in the lab the rest of that day, so I went straight to my apartment to allow my mind to soak in the great news. The thought of winding up my PhD journey in the next six months caused me unexplainable eager anticipation. From that day onwards, my worries shifted from 'How do I prepare for more experimental tests?' to 'How do I draft my thesis?' As I came to understand much later, you don't need to do all the research in the world to get a PhD. You don't need to solve every problem to earn your PhD. You just need to do enough. Since enough is relative, your advisor will help you figure out if you have done enough to warrant a PhD. And like a friend would constantly remind me whenever I felt insecure about my work and whether I had contributed enough to my field, 'Sometimes, the best thesis is a completed thesis.' I'm reminded of what Dr Malika Grayson writes in *Hooded:*

> Advancing the field doesn't mean that you need to think of a completely new concept...it can mean advancing the field one or more steps beyond where it was or adding something new to the existing field. It can also include expanding on someone else's research by unlocking a previously unexplored concept.[14]

An article in *The Guardian*, titled "How Not to Get a PhD", also reminds us of the dangers of overestimating what is required to earn a PhD.

> The words used to describe the outcome of a PhD project—'an original contribution to knowledge'—may sound rather grand, but we must remember that the work for the degree is essentially a research training process and the term 'original contribution' has perforce to be interpreted quite narrowly. It does not mean an enormous breakthrough which has the subject rocking on its foundations, and research students who think that it does will find the process pretty debilitating.[15]

Having committed to a taut deadline and psychologically prepared my advisor, I rolled up my sleeves and went to work. My proposed thesis submission deadline of June 2019 meant I needed to submit a draft to my advisor at least two months before June. I set that deadline to be the end of April. Most of my core chapters had been peer-reviewed and published in high-profile journals. I had also presented my research in three international conferences. And my advisor had read my research papers countless times before I submitted them for publication in the journals and conference proceedings. The research papers gave me a convenient starting point for drafting my thesis. And I was so happy that I had spent some time writing them. I can't imagine how challenging thesis drafting would have been had I not attempted to publish in the journals and conference proceedings.

The months between mid-December 2018 and April 2019 were the most memorable months of my entire PhD. Those months aroused a dense mix of feelings. Whenever I look back, I still shudder over the amount of work and pressure I went through during those months. I will never forget Christmas Day 2018 because I spent the entire day at Linacre Library drafting my thesis. I had gone to Lincare College (one of Oxford's colleges) to celebrate Christmas with my friends from the University of Oxford African Society. As I waited for the event to start, I asked my friend Ruthie, who was a Linacre College student, to show me where their library was. As any PhD student can relate to, I always carried my laptop, a pen, and a book with me everywhere I went, including to most parties. Usually, I would be coming to the event from the lab, or I'd be heading there afterwards. That Christmas Day, I ended up working the whole day and part of that night in the library. I would occasionally rush downstairs to grab a bite with my friends, strike a brief mindless conversation, and rush back to work. During those times, I cared less about holidays. All days were the same in my mind. I had a tight deadline to meet, and I was planning to do all I could to meet the ambitious promises I had made to myself and my advisor. I couldn't wait to submit my thesis and be done with the gruelling PhD journey.

In retrospect, I would have gone insane had it not been for two antidotes that magically appeared in my life. First, in April 2019, I flew to New York to attend the final selection interview for the Schmidt Science Fellows. A day later, I was informed that I had been selected as one of the twenty fellows that year. I had gone through a rigorous selection process that lasted almost one year. Although, based on their criteria, I knew I was qualified to be a fellow, I was well aware of the fellowship's high profile and the competition it attracted. When I was officially informed I had been selected as a fellow, I was beside myself with joy. It meant I officially had a high-profile fellowship awaiting me at the end of my PhD. It also gave me the stamp of confidence I direly needed. As any PhD student knows, a PhD journey has a way of gradually erasing the ink from the original stamp of hubris you had. Having something exciting to look forward to after the journey gives you a boost of confidence and energy you badly need at the end of your journey. I will talk more about intentionally lining up an exciting after-PhD activity or job later in this chapter.

Secondly, in February 2019, I met a charming gentleman and quickly fell in love. He may be another reason those final months leading up to my thesis draft submission are still vividly etched in my mind. My then-boyfriend was working as a researcher at the university, and he would give me much-appreciated company as I toiled away in the library (mostly Radcliffe Science Library, which had become my second home). Sitting next to him in the library gave me more energy and enthusiasm for what I was doing. The overpowering excitement of young love magically dissolved most of my thesis-writing stress. To further push me into meeting the daunting deadline, my boyfriend and I booked a weekend vacation in Europe in early May to celebrate my thesis submission at the end of April. That meant I had to submit my thesis before the vacation. Thanks to the power of setting tight deadlines and shooting for the moon, I submitted my first thesis draft on 1 May 2019. However, I submitted the final thesis three months later than I had planned—September instead of June. And my viva voce was scheduled for 6 December 2019. Needless to say, not everything went according to plan, so I wasn't able to meet my precise deadlines, but committing myself to a tight thesis submission deadline and announcing it to the people I deeply cared about and respected—my family, advisor, and close friends—is the reason I was able to complete my PhD in December 2019. Without this commitment device, I strongly believe my journey would have stretched out a bit longer.

Even years after my PhD was done, I still remind myself that inspiration is perishable. So, as soon as I commit myself to do something, I set a commitment device. A recent case in point is when I got the inspiration to write this book. To set my commitment device, I announced the plan to my friend, Ruthie. Over time, as I drafted the manuscript, I occasionally felt low on energy, lost my inspiration, and would go many weeks without working on it. Whenever I caught up with Ruthie, she would ask, 'No pressure, but how is your new book coming along?' That simple question was enough to refuel my inspiration and jolt me back to work.

I've found that embracing occasional instantaneous inspiration and committing myself to the challenge is quite powerful. Once I start on a project, I seem to discover, albeit scattered over time, guides, tips, and ideas on how to drive the project forward. For example, when I decided to write this book, it was initially daunting to stare at the empty pages of the Google Doc I had titled, 'The PhD Journey: Five Essentials to Have in Mind.' I had no idea where to begin. I knew without any doubt that I was going to write the book, but I had no idea where to begin. A few days later, I returned to the empty Google Doc page and wrote five random themes that I thought summarised the entire journey to my PhD. The initial working title and chapters acted as my guide; they were my skeleton, my sketch, my map. Coming up with the skeleton was the toughest part of the whole writing process. Writing, rewriting, and editing was difficult, but not as tough as getting underway.

Once the rough book skeleton was solidly in place, all I needed were chunks of meat, muscles, and all the other organs, and later some attractive dressing to cover my skeleton. The result? The beautiful (hopefully, that is how you see it) creature you are now holding in your hands. What amazed me was that once I had laid out the working title and chapters (needless to say, these went through amelioration), the content seemed to magically appear everywhere I looked; from some of the books I read (at some point, I had to restrain myself from adding any more references because this book was starting to read like the literature review section of my thesis) and from the conversations I had with my friends.

Robert Masello, in his book *Robert's Rules of Writing*, explains this interesting process:

> [O]nce you make a decision and pick one project and stick to it, you'll notice something strange happens...you become a virtual magnet for related information and ideas. Suddenly, you'll start discovering, all around you, all sorts of juicy tidbits—observations, quotes, statistics, stories—that directly relate to, and nicely amplify, the project you are working on.[16]

Therefore, on the days when you run low on inspiration, just go to your favourite working environment—cafe, library, park— and try to work. Start laying out your rough thesis chapter. Lay out your thesis structure. Edit some of your previous work. Start drafting a conference paper. And when you blank out or tire, come to a full stop, pause, and take a break. If you succeed in doing this, congratulations! Because you have just 'magne-tised yourself' as Robert Masello puts it. From now on, while you walk, eat, converse, or play, without even realising it, your brain will be like a bot, continuously scanning your environment for information, ideas, and themes related to your work. It will be scanning for related dots needed to connect with the previous ones. And so, even when (especially when) motivation and inspi-ration are running low, what you need to do is just start. After all, what you need to initiate your thousand-step journey is that one single baby step. As Confucius says, 'The man who moves a mountain begins by carrying away small stones'.

You have to start from somewhere. You have to initiate a baby step. You'll feel paralysed at times while trying to draft a conference paper, trying to formulate hypotheses, trying to start experiments, trying to draft your thesis. My advice is just start, and along the way, you might gather some motivation and inspi-ration. As Pablo Picasso wisely advised, 'Inspiration exists, but it has to find you working.' Robert Masello adds:

> Sometimes, you'll feel inspired when you sit down to write—and sometimes you won't. That's just the way it is. But sit down you must, and write you will.... The muse is most effectively summoned by the clicking of your keyboard.... Once you stop worrying about where the muse is and focus instead on doing the work at hand, you are most likely to receive a visit...the aroma of hard work draws it [muse] like a bear to honey.[17]

Often, that paper, experiment, or thesis draft won't be impec-cable, but just start working on it, get feedback, and improve it. In regards to embracing the imperfection inherent in any writing, author Anne Lamott, in a TED talk titled "12 Truths I Learned from Life and Writing", says:

Every writer you know writes really terrible first drafts, but they keep their butt in the chair. That's the secret of life. That's probably the main difference between you and them. They just do it. They do it by prearrangement with themselves. They do it as a debt of honour. They tell stories that come through them one day at a time, little by little.[18]

Robert Masello adds, 'Cherish your malcontent status, and remember: The best writers are always striving, however impossibly, for perfection'.[19] Your PhD journey will force you to embrace imperfections. From experience, I can confidently tell you that you will not achieve perfection with your PhD. Always aim to give your best, aim to constantly improve, and aim for growth. Do your best research, write to the best level you can, and then force yourself to come to a full stop; submit and defend your thesis. Because, as you will realise, there will always be something to be improved on, something that could be redesigned, a point of view or perspective that was missed. It helps to remember that a PhD isn't a final product; rather, it's a long, sometimes tortuous, but overall rewarding growth and learning process. To help you efficiently manage your PhD project, you could adopt the four-step project management style: Plan-Do-Check-Act. Charles Kiefer and Leonard A. Schlesinger, in their book *Just Start*, call it the 'Act, Learn, Build, So You Can Act Again' approach. And James Clear refers to it as 'try, fail, learn and try differently'.

When faced with a complex situation or project, we tend to get stuck on the planning part much longer than necessary. James Clear warns, 'It's easy to get bogged down trying to find the optimal plan for change...we are so focused on figuring out the best approach that we never get around to taking action'.[20] Looking back at my PhD journey, I regret spending too much time at the planning stage, obsessively trying to make everything

110 percent ready before moving to the next step. I spent sleepless nights trying to perfect one specific research paper, only to receive major corrections in almost every paragraph when my supervisor reviewed it. Lesson: plan, do (quickly draft that research paper), check (review the results/feedback), and then act on the results/feedback. Only much later, towards the end of my PhD, did it dawn on me that I would have saved so much time and energy had I followed the try-fail-learn-try-differently approach.

4.2 Create immunity for fear and imposter syndrome

Fear and imposter syndrome were my constant companions. In the first years of my PhD journey, they unfailingly accompanied me everywhere I went. Even on the days I wanted to be alone, they tenaciously appeared. They were such a big part of my life that I dedicated a whole chapter in my book *The Bold Dream* to these two notorious companions. Only way later in the journey did I learn a ruse that helped me peacefully coexist with my companions. On the days they insisted on coming along to my presentations, they weren't allowed to raise their hands and ask questions. We had mutually agreed they would sit in a corner, out of my sight, and patiently wait for me to finish my presentation. Then they could shout all they wanted on the way home. I'm happy to report my relationship with these two companions, fear and imposter syndrome, has significantly improved, and we now enjoy a peaceful, healthy relationship.

My struggle with fear and imposter syndrome was exacerbated by two issues: Firstly, I was taking one of the biggest leaps in my academic journey; transitioning from a bachelor's degree from a relatively small university in Kenya to a PhD in one of the finest institutions in the world. Adjusting to a research life at one of the best institutions was no mean feat. I always felt like I had no idea what I was doing. It felt like everyone around me had it all figured out. I'd occasionally interact with some students who, from how they would talk, swagger, and articulate their well-thought-out post-PhD career goals, instantly made you feel like an utter imposter. Looking back now, I wish someone had reminded me that there was no need to shrink in their presence—that it was okay to start from the zero side of the research scale (although I think I started from the negative side of the scale). I wish I had been reminded that most skills in the PhD journey—writing research papers, managing references, reviewing litera-ture—can be easily learnt. I wish I had been reminded that with sufficient time and effort and close mentorship from my advisor, I'd doubtlessly catch up.

Secondly, being a minority student in my lab at that time, I would occasionally doubt my abilities. Over time, though, as I settled in the lab, and became more confident in my abilities, fear and imposter syndrome would go hibernating. But they would be episodically brought back to a healthy life. I remember countless times when I was mistaken for support staff at some of the major conferences I attended. One poignant experience that has refused to leave my mind happened when I was attending a large turbomachinery conference. I always felt foreign in those conferences. I would always, amidst a sea of white male faces, crane my neck, scanning for people who looked like me. There were barely any. One morning, as I pushed my way up the aisle to grab a space at the front of the auditorium, a fellow student a few steps ahead took the last gulp of his coffee, turned, and handed me his cup. Momentary confusion filled both our faces. But it didn't take long for me to realise what was happening since, sadly, it was not the first time I had encountered this kind of situation. My fellow student had mistaken me for a waitress. At that moment, I realised my conference ID wasn't hanging on my neck. Without exchanging a single word, I took out my confer-ence badge and hung it on my neck. The look on his face is still

etched in my memory. He was astounded. While he was struggling to collect appropriate words to apologise, I was already
striding up the aisle. It had happened too many times: someone
handing me their coat, empty coffee cup, or wine glass.

I didn't fit most people's mental picture of an engineer. In
one seminar exclusively organised for engineering students,
someone asked me what my field was. When I answered 'engineering' (what else was I doing in an engineering seminar?), they
shamelessly replied that I didn't look like an engineer. These
unfortunate incidents would instantly set imposter syndrome
free from hibernation. In those moments, I felt displaced, like
I was in the wrong place. Moments like those screamed in my
face that I didn't belong there. With time, I realised that until
the system changed and the engineering environment became
more diverse, I needed to brace myself for a turbulent ride
ahead.

I wish I could tell you the occasional insecurities and
imposter syndrome inherent in a PhD journey will fade away,
but I would be lying. I had expected that insecurities about my
research would abate as I neared the end of earning my PhD.
But even with thousands of data points collected and research
papers written, I still felt I hadn't done enough ground-breaking
research. Only after I had a candid conversation with a friend
did I realise most students battled insecurities throughout their
research journeys. I remember feeling as muddled as ever in my
fourth year of my PhD journey as I began to write up my thesis.
I had so much data from computer simulations and experiments
I had conducted, but they all seemed to make no sense. On the
first day of drafting my thesis, I sat at my desk for hours with no
significant progress. After a while, I decided to pack my bag
and cycle back to my apartment. At my apartment, I opened
the door quietly and tiptoed upstairs to my room, hoping not
to run into one of my housemates. I didn't have the bandwidth
to strike up a conversation. Upstairs, I dropped my bag on the

floor, crawled into my bed, and threw my warm blankets over my head. The plan was to take a power nap. Power naps always calmed my nerves. Whenever I had a million thoughts racing through my mind and couldn't work productively, naps would magically reset my mind. I would nap, then head downstairs and make myself a sugary, milky cup of tea, and my mind would be back in work mode. On that particular day, though, I struggled to nap. After about twenty minutes of tossing and turning, trying very hard to force a nap, I gave up. I scrolled through my phone to find someone I could call to distract myself. A friend I looked up to who had successfully defended his thesis three years earlier came to mind. Without hesitation, I dialled his number.

'I have no energy and enthusiasm to write my thesis', I began whining as soon as we got past our hellos. 'It doesn't feel like I've done meaningful work. Did you ever feel this way?'

'Yes', was his simple answer. I sighed with relief. At least I wasn't alone.

'And', he continued, 'gird yourself because those doubts won't dissipate; they will come in different degrees as you wind up your research. Believe it or not, I still felt doubtful of my research to the day of my defence'. He paused to let that sink into my brain, which was starting to cool down from the whirl of worries.

Our conversation lasted less than ten minutes. But that simple honest confession my friend made about doubting himself and his research, even up to the minute he went in for his PhD defence, changed my life. I sprang up from my bed, threw off my blankets, picked up my bag, and headed straight to my favourite spot at the Radcliffe Science Library. In my favourite corner, I pulled out my laptop and officially began drafting my thesis. When you feel doubtful of your research work, have a candid conversation with trusted friends. The realisation that you aren't the only one battling these feelings will give you the confidence to keep marching forward.

In tackling any major challenge, including embarking on a PhD journey, expect that you will occasionally brush shoulders with fear and imposter syndrome. The bigger the challenge, I've realised, the bigger the fear. What if I fail? What will people say? Fear causes us to over-imagine things and over-analyse situations. As a result, we waste mental energy putting out imaginary fires. Sometimes, we are timid even when we have no reason at all to be. Motivational speaker Les Brown tells a funny story about a fearful man who'd bolt every time he passed by a particular dog that fiercely barked at him. Tired of running, one day he decided he would kick the dog if it attempted to bite him. As he had expected, the dog barked ferociously as it charged at him. He was agitated but determined. As the dog drew closer, his heart beat even faster. When the dog was close enough, the man noticed something funny—the dog had no teeth! All the fear he'd harboured for years melted away like vapour in the sun. But he was embarrassed. He'd been running scared from a toothless dog. In our lives, we are always running, sometimes from toothless dogs.

As I wrote in *The Bold Dream*, one secret to handling fear is making peace with the worst-case scenario. As I prepared to embark on my PhD journey, my worst-case scenario was failing the first-year PhD assessment test. The test marked the transition from a probationary PhD student to a PhD candidate. Only after I made peace with the fact that I had very little to lose, even if I failed the assessment and had to retake it, did I have the confidence to keep moving forward. Julie Norem, a psychology professor at Wellesley College, explains that once people have imagined the worst-case scenarios 'they feel more in control'.[21] I think that is exactly what happened in my case. One year into the PhD program, I passed the assessment test and was officially a PhD candidate. At that point, I wished I had spent less time obsessing about how to put out imaginary fires. The worst-case scenarios never happened, reminding me of what Mark Twain once said, 'I am an old man and have known many troubles, but most of them never happened.'

Fear will feel paralysing sometimes. In those moments, I hope you remember that if you don't pursue your grand idea because of fear, sooner or later, you'll end up dealing with its closest cousin: regret. There is no winning. At some point, you have to decide which one—fear or regret—you are willing to take a chance with. It's affirming to know that even the greatest achievers, leaders, and entrepreneurs have battled this monster called fear at one point or another. Phil Knight, in his memoir *Shoe Dog*, writes, 'You run and run, mile after mile, and you never quite know why. You tell yourself that you're running towards some goal, chasing some rush, but really you run because the alternative, stopping, scares you to death'.[22] I remember so many times when the idea of writing this book had established indestructible roots deep in my mind and heart, that I battled fear: What if I don't get enough content? Will my PhD journey stories be relatable? What if no one buys the book? But what option did I have? To suppress the idea, and never share my stories? That wasn't the best option either. I never wanted to regret never having tried. And so, even in times when I was completely drenched in fear and imposter syndrome, I made one baby step at a time. I wrote one sentence, then the next. And the result? Well, the book you're holding in your hands.

To help with managing relentless doses of fear, it might help to view your PhD as a work-in-progress, not a finished product. And as Jacques Barzun advises, 'Convince yourself that you are working in clay, not marble, on paper not eternal bronze: Let that first sentence be as stupid as it wishes'.[23] That way, you feel liberated to experiment more, you'll be okay with making mistakes, and you'll feel free to voice your opinions. In the process, you become a better researcher and learner. But if you look at it from the point of view that your PhD must be pristine, you'll be more hesitant to experiment and make mistakes.

Sir Ken Robinson, in his TED talk 'Do Schools Kill Creativity?' discusses how kids are unafraid of being wrong; they will give it a go even if they fail, but they lose that capacity as they grow up. Why? Sir Robinson argues that as we grow older, we develop a fear of being wrong. He goes on to warn us, 'If you aren't prepared to be wrong, you'll never come up with anything original.'[24] It also helps to remember that the largest chunk of your PhD journey is spent wading through the uncomfortable and insecure phase of self-doubt, which Abraham Maslow termed the phase of conscious-incompetence. Abraham Maslow's four stages of learning are:

1. **Unconscious-incompetence:** When we don't know that we don't know. Expect to be in this phase at the beginning of your PhD journey.

2. **Conscious-incompetence:** A phase where we are aware of what we don't know. This realisation injects a great deal of insecurity and self-doubt into your system. Expect to spend most of the early stages of your PhD in this phase.

3. **Conscious-competence:** After uncovering what we don't know, we begin to search for answers. We educate ourselves. We gain valuable skills. This could occur at the later stages of your PhD journey.

4. **Unconscious-competence:** We get the answers to what we didn't know before. We become the field experts. We are now knowledgeable and we're even unconscious of our competencies. Hopefully, at the end of your PhD journey, you arrive at this sweet phase that is the apex of the learning stages.[25]

4.3 Assemble crucial tools for the journey ahead

You are about to embark on a long and arduous journey. Carve out some time, in the beginning, to intentionally plan for the journey ahead. Abraham Lincoln has been famously attributed as saying, 'If I had five minutes to chop down a tree, I'd spend the first three sharpening my axe'. Take some time in the beginning to sharpen your axe. Think of a time when you had an important long road trip. What did you do a few days before the trip? You meticulously planned for it. You packed extra clothes. You got some snacks and drinks. You packed extra tires. Similarly, the PhD journey you are about to start will feel like a long trip.

Following are eight activities you can do to prepare.

1. **Take workshops on essay writing, research paper writing, research presenting, etc.** The PhD journey is inherently filled with writing and presentations. You'll be writing research papers and sometimes even grant proposals. You'll have to orally present your research findings. And, ultimately, you'll be required to write a coherent thesis detailing your PhD research work. Most institutions will offer these courses for free or at subsidised prices. I attended countless workshops during the early stages of my PhD journey. The workshops I took included Foundations for a Successful DPhil, Research Skills Toolkit workshops, Scientific Writing: Getting Your Paper Published, Scientific Research Writing for Non-Native English Speakers, Preparing for Learning and Teaching at Oxford: Tutors and Class Assistants, Presentation Skills for Beginners, and Science Writing for Non-Native Speakers among others. The invaluable skills—writing, speaking, presentation, project management skills—that I gained from these workshops have been so helpful even beyond my PhD that I still utilise them to date.

2. **Attend some extra classes**. As a university policy, some universities might require you to complete compulsory course units and earn credits. Even if that isn't a requirement at your university, it will help to attend some of the classes related to your research. My research was in thermofluids, so I took some classes related to thermofluids: Heat and Mass Transfer, Applied Fluid Mechanics, and Engineering Thermodynamics course units. From October 2016 to October 2018, I tutored engineering undergraduate students at Oriel College (one of the University of Oxford's colleges). Tutoring these courses boosted my foundational knowledge of thermofluids. If possible, attend classes that arouse your interest in other topics, even those not related to your work. A friend attended all sorts of lectures, including philosophy and theology. I admired that greatly. In retrospect, I wish I had stretched out of my comfort zone a little bit and attended lectures that had nothing to do with engineering.

3. **Learn from predecessors.** Actively network across departments/universities. Talk with other PhD students. The friendships/networks you form now might help you even after you earn your PhD. You don't have to reinvent the wheel. Learn from your predecessors. They can advise you on what to anticipate in the journey. That way, you can channel your limited energies on improving the wheel instead of reinventing it. This advice comes with the caveat that sometimes people may project their frustrations and fears; consequently, they may end up scaring and limiting you and your imagination. Always seek advice, but be aware that their advice has been shaped by their unique lived experiences. Your situation and experiences might turn out differently.

4. Create a strategy for eating your elephant. We all have a unique style of working. And as I will discuss later, the PhD journey is unique to you, so don't try to blindly copy other people's way of working. I wish I had intentionally taken the time to learn my working style (and stuck to it) at the beginning of my PhD. I later found one study tool that helped me a great deal with getting work done and feeling good about my progress. Sticking to a SMART (specific, measurable, attainable, relevant, and time-based) weekly to-do list—like the one shown in Figure 4.3.1—boosted my productivity. By writing the SMART weekly to-do list, you commit to trying your best to complete only the activities on the list. This helps you break down a gigantic list of tasks that need to be completed during the year or semester into small, easily manageable chunks of work. I found the to-do list helpful in terms of pinning me down to concentrate all my efforts on a specific portion of my work at a time.

Fig 4.3.1: An example of my weekly to-do list

Week of Monday 8 June 2018

1. Draft ASME conference paper.

- Focus mostly on the methodology and discussion.

2. Set up ANSYS Fluent simulation for the 3D model.

- Run two parameters, and analyse the results.

3. Fill and submit the Graduate Self-Assessment form.

4. Fill out the grant application for the 2020 ASME conference.

You must have heard this quirky question before: How do you eat an elephant? The answer is: One bite at a time! The PhD journey is exactly like eating an elephant. You have to concentrate on one bite at a time. Don't try to figure out everything at once; you'll be overwhelmed. A mini to-do list—with tasks broken down to one year, six months, one month, or one week—allows you to do just that; eat the elephant one bite at a time. This simple to-do list also helped me to feel I was constantly making some progress. There was evidence of that progress written down and ticked (with a red pen) at the end of the week, month, or semester. Another way that might help you reduce procrastination and efficiently eat your elephant is setting periodic milestones or targets with your advisor. That way, even if you become lazy and run out of motivation at some point (which will happen so many times), the deadlines and milestones will administer periodic doses of adrenaline, which is always enough to expel any trace of laziness.

5. **Develop a strategy for managing large documents.** You are going to embark on a long, drawn-out journey, and at the end, you'll have vast written materials—thesis rough drafts, publications, or anything else related to research. It'll help you immeasurably to dedicate some time at the beginning of your PhD to learn (if you aren't already familiar with) some large-document-handling software. I spent most of my evenings and weekends over the Trinity term (one of Oxford's terms, running from April to June) of 2017 learning how to use LaTex. LaTex is a software system for document preparation. It is particularly helpful for writing and revising a large document. You can access its online version through the Overleaf website: https://www.over-leaf.com. LaTex syphoned a chunk of time from my already packed PhD schedule, and I had to miss out on some

exciting social stuff. But LaTex made my life easier later in the journey when drafting, rewriting, and editing my thesis. At that time, I didn't regret a single minute I had invested in learning the software.

6. **Manage references/literature.** Throughout your PhD journey, you'll read and collect innumerable literature materials. To avoid unnecessary stress later when trying to locate a crucial paper/reference as you write your thesis or prepare for defence, skillfully organise your literature materials from the onset. So many reference management software programs exist that will help you easily store and retrieve your references, including Zotero, Endnote, Mendeley, Sciwheel, RefWorks, JabRef, and Paperpile. Whichever you decide to employ, ensure it works for you and your research. My advisor once shared with me a simple literature collection Excel spreadsheet template that forever transformed how I conducted a literature review. A simplified example of this Excel spreadsheet is shown in Table 4.3.1. Employing this kind of spreadsheet forced me to pay close attention to key methodology, data, and results (since I had to summarise these in the spreadsheet) from whichever literature paper I read. Using this strategy brought much more enthusiasm into the literature review process, which can sometimes be boring and monotonous. Plus, the spreadsheet acted as tangible evidence of the progress I was making in my PhD, so it boosted my confidence. It was always daunting (more so in the beginning) when I didn't have any physical evidence of my progress at the end of the week, month, or semester.

Table 4.3.1: A literature matrix I used to record key information from literature review materials

Paper details	Andrews, G. E., et al. "Transpiration Cooling: Contribution of Film Cooling to the Overall Cooling Effectiveness." International Journal of Turbo and Jet Engines 3.2-3 (1986): 245-256.
Type of study	Experimental
Brief study procedure	• Cross flow gases at **27 m/s and 750 K** were used. • The main aim of this study was to investigate the **influence of the transpiration wall** characteristics.
Material employed	• **Porosint Rigid Mesh** - a porous stainless steel manufactured in sheets by rolling and sintering layers of stainless steel wire mesh.
Coolant used	Compressed air at room temperature
Conclusion	• Pressure loss **doesn't influence** the coolant mixture in a **porous wall** unlike in full coverage discrete hole film cooling. • To eliminate **jet stirring**, a large number of **small dia holes** should be used. • Higher coolant flow rates **didn't promote** turbulent mixing in **transpiration cooling.** • **Film cooling** is a **big contributor** to the overall cooling at all coolant flow rates.
Remarks	Relevant to my work.

7. **Read books on strategies, tips, and tricks for thriving in a PhD journey.** A ton of books exist that you could read to gain some insights into what to expect during your PhD journey. You will learn some strategies that others have employed in the past to successfully thrive and excel in the journey. Below are some books that might interest you.

- *How to Write a Thesis* by **Rowena Murray**. In this book, Professor Murray gives you in-depth information on what to include in important sections of your thesis, such as the introduction, results, and conclusion. After writing a draft of my thesis, I wasn't very sure whether I had included all the details. Because of Professor Murray's valuable advice, suggestions, and practical tips, I was able to breeze through writing some sections of my thesis like the introduction.

- *How to Survive Your PhD* by **Jason R. Karp**. I love reading other people's stories. In this book, Dr Karp candidly shares his PhD journey stories and experiences. He takes us through the most important topics in a PhD journey, including finances, choosing the right institution, and choosing the right advisor. I particularly liked Dr Karp's practical advice and examples—for both the scientific and non-scientific disciplines—on how you should write some important sections of a thesis such as the introduction, literature review, results, discussion.

- *Writing Your Dissertation in Fifteen Minutes a Day: A Guide to Starting, Revising and Finishing Your Doctoral Thesis* by **Joan Bolker**. Aside from giving you some practical tips on how to stay disciplined throughout the writing and revising phases of your thesis, Bolker also gives you some tips on choosing a research topic and an advisor.

- *Writing the Winning Thesis or Dissertation: A Step-by-Step Guide* **by Randy L. Joyner, William A. Rouse, and Allan A. Glatthorn.** These authors give useful tips on, among other topics, laying the groundwork for your thesis and scheduling your thesis project.

8. **Figure out how to back up your work.** Find out which options are available for you to constantly back up your data. As you progress in the journey, you will collect countless materials, including your notes, computer data, thesis drafts, etc. In the unfortunate event that your machine crashes or your lab building catches fire, you want to be on the safe side with your data safely backed up so you can easily retrieve it. It also helps to have some copies of any huge document you're working on. One particular week, I was editing a document called ConferenceXPaper_10Apr2020. I would copy and save the better draft after a week or so under the name ConferenceXPaper_17Apr2020. This way I was able to revert to some previous versions in case I lost my current document, or if it crashed. Also, occasionally when I made a major editing mistake while working on the current document, I could revert to the previous version to save my day.

4.4 Waste time creatively

Are the experiments not going as planned? Are you not getting the results you were hoping for? Are you feeling clouded and muddled? Instead of feeling guilty and useless, take an hour, a day, a weekend, or a week off. Try non-research-related activities that aren't mentally engaging—activities that you enjoy doing that will reinvigorate you. They can be as simple as taking a long saunter, going for a jog, playing the piano, watching a movie, taking a micro-vacation, or going to dinner with friends. You'll find that when you go back to your work, you'll have different perspectives and ideas on how to solve your problem. According to Heracleous and Robson in their article "Why Procrastination Can Help Fuel Creativity," research has shown that deliberate productive procrastination and wasting time creatively can boost efficiency and innovation.[26] In his book *In Praise of Wasted Time*, Alan Lightman fervently champions the idea of wasting time, especially when you get stuck. From his research, he discovered that the decisive factor to enhancing creativity and innovation seemed to be introducing intentional procrastination between periods of focused thinking. Creativity and innovation occurred when some time was taken off work to permit some space and time to ponder a problem at a leisurely and subconscious level. For the unconscious mind to work on the problem at hand, however, the mind must be seeded with that particular problem before starting the procrastination phase. Lightman reminds us that what we view as procrastination or avoidance of the problem might actually be a beneficial use of our time and minds. After an extensive analysis of some of the grand scientific discoveries of the twentieth century, he uncovered four crucial stages that underlie all these discoveries: 1) preparation, 2) being stuck, 3) new insight or change of perspective, and 4) discovery. He suggests that we shouldn't dread being stuck, but instead welcome it since it catalyses the creative imagination. So, if your experiment, dissertation draft, or fieldwork isn't going as you planned and you feel stuck, take a break. Redirect your mind to something else, perhaps one of your hobbies; procrastinate with intentionality and allow the problem to incubate in the unconscious mind.

To further encourage you to close your laptop and take some time off from your work, here is Maya Angelou's advice on taking a break to rejuvenate. In her essay "A Day Away", Angelou tells us about how she gave herself a day away once a year or so, and how that one day away invigorated her. She advocates that each person deserves a day away in which no problems are confronted, no solution searched for. She writes:

Each of us needs to withdraw from the cares which will not withdraw from us. We need hours of aimless wandering or spates of time sitting on park benches.... When I return home, I am always surprised to find some questions I sought to evade had been answered and some entanglements I had hoped to flee had become unraveled in my absence. A day away acts as a spring tonic. It can dispel rancor, transform indecision, and renew the spirit.[27]

Another ruse I employed to help me recharge and be productive during my PhD journey was taking micro-vacations. I found I was the most productive when I had exciting micro-vacations to look forward to. Most of these micro-vacations were possible courtesy of soccer and track meets. Most of my fondest memories from my PhD time came while visiting different cities and universities across the UK, from Glasgow to Cardiff, through my active involvement in the Varsity-level soccer and track events. Through these sporting activities and tours, I got a golden opportunity to meet and network with students from other universities whom I couldn't have met otherwise. Take advantage of clubs that will force you to take time off work. Attend conferences that will offer you an opportunity to briefly escape the intense university environment to recharge and network.

In In Praise of Wasted Time, Lightman describes the difference between chronos and Kairos time, a distinction worth remembering on your PhD journey. Lightman states:

Chronos is clock time...Chronos is quantitative time...a relentless time that marches on mindlessly in the external world, oblivious to the lives of human beings. Kairos, on the other hand, is time created by events, often human events.... It might be the duration of a season, or of a meal, or of a love affair. When an event of human significance occurs, it occupies a great deal of kairos.... Kairos time is forever. It is the time of memory. It is the time of being.[28]

Most of your PhD journey milestones will be dictated by time that is out of your control. You might not be able to change your university's policy on when to transition from one level of PhD to the next. You might not have control over when your scholarship will run out. If you plan to attend a particular conference, the conference paper submission deadlines will be largely out of your control. Although in some cases, you might request an extension, or exemption, by and large, these deadlines and milestones are fixed and out of your control. From time to time, you'll have to adjust your schedule to meet them. But while you meticulously pay attention to these milestones, I hope you don't completely sacrifice kairos. Unforgettable fond memories and long-lasting friendships will be created through kairos.

4.5 If you don't ask, you'll never know

I panicked when I realised most of my PhD work would involve using a fluid simulation software called ANSYS Fluent. I hardly knew how to operate the software. I researched where I could get a crash course on how to use it. The biggest challenge was the cost of the courses; two courses I wanted to take cost more than £1000 combined, and I couldn't afford to cover the cost using my scholarship stipend. So, I asked my advisor if I could get some financial support for the courses. I showed him all the research I had conducted—course dates, costs, etc. He was pleased that I had come to him with a problem and possible solutions. He asked me to fill out some forms requesting funding. I got the request approved, and I ended up attending the two online courses, one over Christmas 2015 and the other over Easter break 2016. The skills, tips, and tricks I learnt from those online courses helped me a great deal not only during my PhD but also post-PhD. If I hadn't volunteered that I barely knew how to use the software, my advisor might not have known and I might have struggled alone.

Don't be shy to take charge of your research by proactively seeking ways to improve your skills. Be resourceful in noting some courses and materials you need for your PhD. It took me quite some time, perhaps till the end of my second year, to realise I wasn't an undergrad anymore. Only then was I confident enough to respectfully say 'no' to activities or suggestions that didn't fit into the grand scheme of things in regards to my PhD. Even though you get supervision and advice from your advisor regarding your PhD, by and large, your PhD is your research. You tend to start out being dependent on your advisor, doing what they suggest, following their schedule, etc. But with time, you are supposed to grow into an independent researcher. Learn to respectfully say 'no' and offer your point of view, regarding things that have a direct impact on your PhD— its direction, implication, and duration.

Asking questions and being proactive doesn't stop with your research. Is there a conference/research grant you would like to apply for, but you are unsure whether you qualify? Just ask. Are you unsure if you've done enough to graduate? Just ask. If you are struggling to complete your assignment, term paper, or meet any deadline, and would like to get an extension, just ask. I was able to take advantage of a myriad of opportunities just by asking. So many times I would read an email about a particular opportunity and instantly think I didn't meet all the eligibility criteria. Only when I emailed and explained my situation and qualifications did I realise I had a chance. Most rules and regulations aren't cast in stone; they can be amended. Your situation can be contextualised, and your deadline might be extended. If unsure about some policies and rules, just ask; you will save so much time and open lots of possibilities for yourself.

4.6 Have hobbies and a life outside your PhD program

You might love your PhD program with all your heart, but there is a high chance it won't love you back in equal measure. It'll slap you in the face now and then. That's where hobbies (and life outside the PhD journey) will come in handy to help soothe your bruises. Whatever your hobby is, embrace and build upon it. As humans, we have an innate desire to always be useful, to be important. We want to feel we're doing something good with our lives. We want to feel we are making progress. Having hobbies and a life outside your PhD journey will help you use your time wisely and improve other areas of your life, consequently, boosting your confidence and self-esteem and giving you some sense of meaning and accomplishment.

One hobby I'm proud to have explored is reading books not related to my research. I serendipitously stumbled on this habit of reading in 2017 when I went through an episode of emotional distress. I plunged into reading books to distract myself from depressive moods. I would read on the bus on my way to and from the lab. I would read during lunch hours. I would read before bed. It was therapeutic. The more I read, the more I craved to read more. I got addicted and haven't stopped since. Reading has opened vast doors to a world I barely knew. Through reading, my creative and scientific writing has tremendously improved. Some of those books have challenged my view of life. Some have improved my knowledge of money and wealth creation. Reading is a hobby I'd strongly recommend. If you are new to reading, start with easy, captivating reads.

Although I engaged in numerous hobbies during my PhD journey, my favourite was sports. Most of my out-of-lab time was spent in sports. I played soccer for the University of Oxford Furies team (women's second team), and I was a 400 m Blues hurdler. The University of Oxford Blue is the highest honour granted to a sportsperson for competing at the highest level within that sport. As discussed earlier, these sports tours presented a chance for me to recharge and to interact and network with students from other universities I couldn't have met otherwise. When things were bleak in my lab—experiments not running as I had expected, being stuck while drafting my thesis—these sports tours kept me sane. The sporting activities also gave me something more to live for, more than my PhD. There were personal best times I was targeting in the 400-meter hurdles track event. I looked forward to building my soccer skills so that one day I could play for the Blues team. In addition, by having my plate overspilling with activities, I was at my best in my time management game, and I was even more productive. It almost sounds counterintuitive (accomplishing more when you are the busiest), but thanks to Parkinson's Law, this is possible. Parkinson's Law states that work expands to fill the time available for its completion. Since I was out for the sporting events most of the weekends, I had to learn to make the most of every minute I was working on my research. Looking back, it makes sense that I achieved more in my research when my plate was overspilling with hobbies.

If possible, find something you love doing, a hobby you'll occasionally turn to when you want to remind yourself of your worth and your important contribution to this world. That hobby will occasionally take attention away from your research. Make it something that fills you with joy and gives you a sense of purpose. Plus, your hobby—volunteering, writing, painting, sports—might end up becoming a full-fledged career option, or ballooning into something monumental that earns you extra income, awards and recognitions, or raises your profile.

4.7 How do you work best?
We all have a unique way of working. Take time to understand your brain and how you work best. The PhD journey is long, so

you need to establish the routine and work culture that best suit your reading and working style. Ask for advice and read stories of other people, but in the end, cherry-pick only the styles that work best for you. Don't try to blindly copy other students' work culture. I remember feeling guilty every time I left my lab early (sometimes as early as 2 p.m.) to attend sports training. My colleagues would still be busy at the lab working on an experiment, doing computer simulations, or writing conference papers. As I checked out of the lab, I would feel like everyone's eyes were following me through the door, wondering whether I was serious with my PhD. (I'm sure they were too entrenched in their work to even notice, but still, the guilt didn't go away.) I mostly experienced these twitches of guilt in my first year. Later, I came to terms with how we are all very different. The way my colleagues worked was very different from how I worked. They could be night owls, and I could be a morning person. Their passions, dreams, and fears were different from mine. We had a love and passion for different hobbies. Sports energised me; they gave me a sense of accomplishment, some sense of purpose. Some of my friends would wonder why I would brave a bone-chilling winter morning to attend soccer or track training. We are all travelling in different lanes, usually at different speeds and heading to different destinations (having started from different starting points in life). It's much better to know your speed, your destination, and your lane, and stick to your lane.

Not until it dawned on me that I would never work the way my colleagues worked—that I was okay with being me, working the best way I could, and sticking to my lane—did the guilt disappear and I could unapologetically embrace my working style. Sometimes I would even request permission to miss some lab meetings so I could attend key sports events. Thankfully, my supervisor was very supportive and understanding, so I managed to guiltlessly and proudly balance sports with research. Learn who you are and what gives you a sense of meaning and accomplishment. What are you passionate about? What energises you? The earlier you discover your lane and stick to it, the better.

As time went by and I learnt the way my brain worked best, I tweaked my schedule to work only when I was the most efficient. I later discovered I had substantial inertia; it would take ages before my work motivation kicked in at the start of the week. Most of my Mondays were terrible. I got so little done on Mondays. Because of the flexibility I had over my work schedule, I redesigned my work week to start on Tuesday and end on Saturday afternoon. My weekend days were Sunday and Monday. I would use Sunday to catch up with family, connect with friends, go to church, etc. Monday was dedicated to track training. Sports and lab work superbly complemented each other. As I made progress on the track, I felt a sense of progress and accomplishment, and that energy would be transferred to my work in the lab. This balance tremendously boosted my happiness level. If your schedule and circumstances allow, set your routine—a routine that works best for you. Forcing your brain to work just because it is a workday, or because everyone else is working, can be inefficient and draining. Maya Angelou warns, 'Never try to take the manners of another as your own, for the theft will be immediately evident and the thief will appear as ridiculous as a robin with peacock feathers hastily stuck on. Style is as unique and non-transferable and perfectly personal as a fingerprint'.[29] Therefore, strive to establish and stick to your unique working style.

Not only is a PhD program unique and you are unique, but it's important to keep in mind that the journey to a PhD is unique to the country, university, and department administering it. As much as the bottom line of a PhD is to add knowledge to your field, write a doctoral thesis, and successfully defend it, the specific milestones that have to be compulsorily ticked off for you to graduate may vary based on your PhD field of study, university, and country. For instance, a PhD at the University of Oxford, and most universities in the UK, is research-heavy. Therefore, I wasn't required to take any classes to graduate. Although I chose to attend some lectures, I did so purely for knowledge and class experience's sake. By contrast, most universities in the USA are class-intensive, and sometimes you might take up to three years of classes. Research what the process is like in the field, university, and country where you plan to take your doctoral degree so that nothing will get you by surprise. Are you expected to take some classes? If yes, how many and what is the pass mark? Are you required to publish some research papers? If yes, how many publications are you required to publish to graduate? Will you be required to sit for a qualifying exam? Will you be required to teach? What are some major milestones and their timelines? What happens in the worst-case scenario when you miss these deadlines?

4.8 Regularly sharpen your saw

Stephen Covey dedicated a whole chapter in his acclaimed book *The 7 Habits of Highly Effective People* to a crucial habit of continuous improvement. He named this habit, Habit 7: Sharpen the Saw. To attain a sustainable, long-term, and effective lifestyle, Covey argues that we should strive to balance and renew our resources, energy, and health. He reminds us that this habit of continuous improvement entails:

> preserving and enhancing the greatest asset you have—you. It's renewing the four dimensions of your nature—physical (e.g., through exercise, nutrition, stress management), spiritual (e.g., through meditation), mental (e.g., through reading, writing) and social/emotional (e.g., through service, empathy).[30]

Covey correctly points out that we often run into the temptation of ignoring these important saw-sharpening activities like
recreation, healthy eating, and relationship building because
they don't seem urgent, at least in comparison to other dead-
line-driven projects we're constantly dealing with. Furthermore,
not always reaping instant benefits from these saw-sharpening
activities only exacerbates our proclivity to ignore or push them
aside. What we don't realise is that these saw-sharpening activities help us to be efficient and more sustainable. If you are
running a sprint in life, you could get away with sacrificing these
saw-sharpening activities, but for marathons—a PhD journey
falls squarely in this category—you can't afford to sacrifice them.

Taking time for rest and unplugging from social media and
technology can help us rest, live in the moment, limit distrac-
tions, and even improve our productivity. The first time I
attempted to unplug from my phone to improve my productivity
was during my thesis writing stage. I would leave my phone at
home and go work in a library. On day one, I barely survived till
lunch hour. I was craving my phone like a drug. The unquench-
able desire overwhelmed me by midday, and I embarrassingly
went back home for the sole purpose of checking my phone.
Despite my unsuccessful first attempt, the effort stretched my
unplugging-from-phone muscle. After some time, I would even
go about a week without checking my phone. While I drafted
my thesis, I even uninstalled WhatsApp from my phone because
it was the most distractive app on my phone. (I was more disciplined with Email, Facebook, and other social media platforms.)
I went without WhatsApp for about two months. The first few
days after weaning myself from WhatsApp, I felt like an addict
trying to recover from drug addiction. This was not surprising
since we all know the dangers of small doses of dopamine that
get released into our bodies every time we receive an email or
text message. Brian Tracy reminds us of the danger of dopamine, 'Each time you respond to the novelty or newness of an

email or a text message, your body releases a shot of dopamine, the same chemical found in cocaine. This dopamine acts as a stimulant and actually gives you a small feeling of pleasure'.[31]

Over time, I totally forgot about my phone and found other activities to fill my time. During this time, I went into a state of absolute productivity and produced what Cal Newport calls 'deep work' (professional activities performed in a state of distraction-free concentration that pushes your cognitive capabilities to their limit).[32] When I submitted my thesis, one reward I had lined up to celebrate my milestone was reinstalling WhatsApp. What surprised me when I reinstalled the app was that in the two months I was away, I hadn't missed it much. The world hadn't stopped. Only a handful of friends had tried contacting me via WhatsApp, and when they couldn't find me, they'd contacted me through other channels like Email. The point is, if your mind feels congested, take time off to breathe. Just alert close important people—family, friends—before you go dark. You'll be surprised how many people care earnestly enough to go the extra mile to reach you when you are unreachable. This creative way of dealing with my work by taking time off from my phone was initially meant to help me complete my PhD, but I've occasionally practised this ritual since then. I now occasionally switch off my phone for a few hours/half a day/a few days without checking it. During that time, I rechannel my attention and energy into some project at hand. Brian Tracy recommends that we treat our brains like a battery that, when used, discharges and burns out over time. He reminds us:

> Just like a cell phone needs to be recharged regularly so that it operates at its highest capability, you need to recharge your brain regularly as well. You need to set aside specific times, and often extended periods of time, to fully recharge your brain battery so that you can be alert and aware most of the time.[33]

4.9 Write research papers/chapter drafts as often as you can

Every year during my PhD journey, I attempted to write at least one conference paper. Many of the papers were accepted for conferences, while one or two weren't. Regardless, all the papers and chapter drafts made my life easier later on as I prepared my thesis draft. You might be lucky enough to be at an institution that allows you to submit a journal format thesis, where your thesis is primarily a compilation of already peer-reviewed journal papers, and the only thing you will need to do is prepare the introduction and conclusion chapters, and then your thesis is done and dusted.

Another tool that helped me a great deal in the later stages of my PhD was keeping a record of all the meetings with my advisor (and the professors who administered my Transfer of Status and Confirmation of Status viva voce). Don't trust your brain to store feedback and everything else discussed in important meetings. Use whatever means accessible that works best for you—note-taking, audio recording, etc. During the first couple of meetings with my advisor, I was soaking in a lot of jargon and was struggling to capture all that we discussed. I would say 'pardon' repeatedly because I was embarrassed by how much I didn't understand. I used to carry my fat, spiral A4 notebook with an emerald-green cover to all our meetings. I would try to capture as much as possible while we discussed my work. Sometimes after these meetings, I would immediately summarize key takeaways in an audio recording on my phone just to be sure I captured and kept all our key discussions.

I had underestimated how much record-keeping would help me later when writing my thesis. As I drafted my thesis, whenever I struggled to remember some details of the work I did in my first year, I would just pull out my slightly tattered spiral A4 notebook from four years back. If the notebook couldn't do the magic of arousing my memory, I would go back to audio recordings. This way of record-keeping saved my life. I advise that you try this too; the earlier you start keeping records of your work, the better. Keep a summary of feedback from key meetings. Keep a record of the decisions and assumptions you make along the way. Earning a PhD is a long process, and you can't rely on your memory to recall all the details of the work you did or assumptions you made, especially in the first years of your PhD. Laura Valadez-Martinez in her 2016 TEDx talk "Things About a PhD Nobody Told You About" says one of the best pieces of advice she ever got during her PhD was to keep important information in a research diary.[34]

I didn't try to capture and record only my discussions with my advisor but also some discussions with my colleagues. I requested permission to record my friend, a fellow PhD student who was my senior, as she outlined for me a long list of how to run an experimental test setup that I was inheriting from her. The experimental setup (the journal Nature wrote a brief feature on my work using this rig[35]) was one of the dangerous setups in the lab—it operated under high pressure and at speeds that caused the air passing through it to produce ear-splitting sounds. I had to sound an alarm at least three times before running any test on it. There were also umpteen lists of other procedures that needed to be followed in a strict order; otherwise, I'd risk causing accidents. The recordings I made on the day my friend gave me a detailed orientation on how to operate the rig were extremely helpful a few months down the line when I needed to repeat some experiments.

4.10 Invest in a quality support system

The PhD journey can feel lonely, especially if you're studying abroad miles away from your comfortable environment and loved ones. As soon as you settle into the journey, be intentional about investing in a dependable bevy of people—friends who will have your back in good and bad times. These friends will be there to hear you rant about your failed experiments, rejected journal articles, etc. They'll be there to hold your hand when your PhD stresses threaten to drown you. They'll celebrate your milestones and achievements. They'll be your support system when going through grief. While you commune with these friends, sharing your home meals and talking about home politics, in your home country's language, you'll feel homesickness fade away. This dependable group of friends will be your family.

Carve out time to hang out and connect with your friends. As I discussed before, the times I spent with friends sharing a meal or doing fun activities were the most memorable of my PhD journey. At the top of my list of fond memories is when we'd go dancing during the most anticipated AfroBOPs. We'd dance our hearts out to African music. And we'd momentarily feel transported back to our home cities. We'd also occasionally go to movies. One movie we watched was *Creed*. I vividly remember this night out with my friends because the energy and inspiration from that movie catapulted us through a grim winter full of academic expectations. Some movies can inspire; *Creed* was one that injected a dose of motivation into the system of a worn-out, final-year PhD student.

If we weren't dancing or watching movies, we would host monthly dinners where my housemates and I would cook Kenyan meals. We would invite our friends for a night of home-cooked food and conversation. We had so many of those monthly fellowships that our friends nicknamed our apartment the Kenya House. Most of my memories of my time at Oxford were formed in that house. The stories, worries, dreams, fears, and various vulnerabilities we shared bonded us deeply. During one of these fellowships, we connected with Dr Elisha Ngetich, a fellow Rhodes Scholar from Kenya who was also pursuing a PhD. While we shared our stories of how we got to Oxford, we were surprised by how much we had in common, including similar financial, academic struggles, and even the same surname, though we are unrelated. We then challenged each other to write a book to inspire students who might be travelling a similar path to ours. That is how I came to co-author *The Bold Dream: Transcending the Impossible*. During one of these fellowships, I also landed myself a boyfriend. Although we parted ways later, we shared a great time. I mentioned earlier how his companionship and friendship became a much-needed anchor at the end of my PhD journey when I was writing my thesis.

Your friends (within and outside your research group) might not offer you all the welfare support you need in the journey. You might need specialised services like counselling therapy that your friends aren't well trained to offer. That is where the department in charge of students' wellbeing (such as the Counselling Service Department) in your university will come in. As you walk on the PhD journey, part of your research should be to find out which wellbeing services (such as counselling therapy) your university offers, how much they cost, and how to access them just in case you need them down the line. In creating this network of support, you might need to put in extra effort, especially if you are a minority student in your department/institution. But the effort you put in will be generously rewarded. During my PhD, I found a supportive community through the Women in Engineering (WiE) group at the department. During WiE social events and fellowships, we'd unreservedly share both bad and good experiences of being minorities in our respective labs. I always walked out of these fellowships feeling like I was coming from counselling therapy. Plus, I made dear friends there whom I still stay in touch with and collaborate with years later post-PhD.

While you tap into your support system, remember to offer your help to other students who might be struggling. Your stories, struggles, and strategies from your PhD journey are precious, and they can help another student who might be in the same boat. Volunteer to share your stories through whatever medium works for you—vlog, blog, book. Even on the days you would rather escape into your cocoon, try your best to help a person or two. J. D. Schramm writes about a life principle one of his colleagues believes in—putting cookies into the jar before you take any out. He advises, 'Build a network by helping others; learn about their needs and priorities, and support their objectives while still getting your work done'.[36]

4.11 Be creative about study locations/ times/routines

Most Saturdays, our lab was quiet because there were fewer students working in the lab on the weekends. As I mentioned earlier, I redesigned my work week to run Tuesday to Saturday— when my brain worked best. I loved working in the lab on Saturdays; I had inexplicable concentration. Saturdays were the most creative days of my PhD time. If I couldn't figure out something during the week and needed laser focus to crack it, I would postpone it to Saturday. Some of my best breakthroughs happened on Saturdays.

Whenever I was low on inspiration for the work at hand, I would simply change my scenery. I still use this trick today. Depending on my mood on a particular day, I would work from a working cafe, lab, or a quiet library. Some cafes have very comfortable working spaces with free Wi-Fi where I'd work comfortably with music on and a cup of coffee by my side. Working from a cafe, I'd feel less intensity and could concentrate for longer periods. But occasionally, I'd prefer a quiet place with a minimum level of noise; in that case, a quiet library would work better than a cafe or lab. Dr Karp notes, 'While sometimes it's helpful to immerse yourself in your familiar environment...other times it's helpful to immerse yourself in a completely foreign environment'.[37] Working from the same lab, same desk, and same building every day for seven days or 365 days can be monotonous and morale-sucking. James Clear advises that 'Motivation is overrated; environment often matters more'.[38] Sometimes when running low on motivation, changing your work environment might help to revive the waning motivation and enthusiasm. James Clear adds:

> 'Given that we are more dependent on vision than any other sense...a small change in what you see can lead to a big shift in what you do. As a result, you can imagine how important it is to live and work in environments that are filled with productive cues and devoid of unproductive ones'.[39]

My friend, Ruthie, took the idea of switching up the work environment to another level. Every time she needed to focus on major work, when she needed to meet a major deadline, she would book an affordable Airbnb nearby and work from there. She would bury herself in her work, then come back to the university feeling utterly revitalised and having completed whatever project she was working on. If you are unable to have occasional work getaways like my friend, you could make use of occasional travels, such as when attending a conference. When I travel to a new place, I take advantage of new scenery/location/time zone to shake up my schedule and be productive.

4.12 Line up an exciting post-PhD activity

The PhD journey can be quite draining. You'll barely have energy and enthusiasm toward the end of the journey. To rejuvenate yourself to complete the process, consider lining up interesting activities to look forward to post-PhD. The post-PhD activity doesn't have to be career-related; it can be something as simple as a one-month vacation. Or it can be something you've been putting aside for a protracted time like volunteering, backpacking, etc. Whatever you're passionate about will help you rekindle motivation at the end of the journey.

I received the Schmidt Science Fellowship during the last months of my PhD. I can't begin to tell you how much this fellowship forced me to quickly tie up any loose ends to my PhD, including writing up and submitting my thesis. Since the fellowship values networking and connection, both intra- and inter-cohort, I was required to begin my postdoctoral research work and other fellowship activities around the same time as my cohort mates. The submission of my PhD stopped being my personal (and my advisor's) business; now other parties cared about my end-of-PhD timeline. Were it not for the pressure from the preset fellowship timelines, I might have taken a few more months (hopefully, not years!) to wind up my PhD. So, if your PhD is dragging on at the end of the journey and your motivation is plummeting, some external factors might help nudge you to wind up your project faster. If for some reason you are unable to have something lined up, that is still fine. Don't let those social media posts from your colleagues who have just submitted their theses (and are travelling around the world, or starting nice jobs) dishearten you. You'll get there.

4.13 Be kind to yourself

Earning a PhD is a continuous learning process. As a result, mistakes and errors are bound to happen. You might make a mistake in designing your experiments, in formulating your hypothesis, etc. You might choose an unsuitable university, research topic, or advisor. Whether or not these mistakes are your fault, be kind to yourself. Learn from the mistakes, adjust, and move on.

Being kind to yourself doesn't stop in the lab; it also applies to your out-of-lab personal life. As you travel down the PhD road, life won't stop. The world around you is moving on as usual. There will be good and bad times. And since we're a part of the world, we aren't insulated from the mixture of emotions that will constantly be thrown at us. When unfortunate events occur, seek help and be kind to yourself. Allow yourself to break down sometimes. Allow yourself to be clueless sometimes. Allow yourself time to heal. The last quarter of 2017 was one of the toughest periods of my life. I was grieving the death of my eldest brother. His loss took me to dark places I had never been before. Grieving my brother's death while miles away from home, from my family, added salt to an already wide-open and delicate wound. During this time, I craved emotional support from my family. With time and constant support from my friends, I healed. If you're going through grief, I hope the following lessons from my grief journey will be helpful.

- **Tap into your support system.** Hopefully, the support system you have built thus far will extend a helping hand in your time of need. You may need to be courageous enough to open up to your friends and let them know you aren't okay and you need their support. My housemates went above and beyond during my grieving process. I remember that on days when I couldn't even cook, my housemates cooked and brought meals up to my room. They cleaned my room and did my laundry. Those who couldn't come to visit me called to check on me periodically. It's also good to remember that not everyone will understand you're going through a rough time.

- **Don't rush the process.** Because of the periodic pang of guilt I felt during the days I was away from the lab attending my brother's funeral, I tried to rush the healing process. I wish I had been a little bit kinder to myself. Understand that grieving is a multistage process with no exact timelines for how long the whole process will take. Grief found me when I barely knew anything about the grieving process. Having a rough idea of the process will help you grieve better. Expect that you'll go through (in no particular order) the five stages of grief: denial, anger, bargaining, depression, and acceptance. And be okay with your healing process possibly taking longer than you anticipate.

- **Seek counselling therapy.** I filled out a form requesting counselling therapy, but I never submitted it. I was scared to acknowledge I was in a very bad place mental health-wise. I regret not taking the courageous step of seeking counselling. My healing process might have been smoother and faster had I seen a therapist. If you are going through loss and grief, please seek help, and unhesitatingly book an appointment with a therapist.

- **Try to fill up the voids within.** Once you have taken ample time to go through the process of grief, it's time to find positive things to fill up the voids within. Personally, sports—soccer and track—renewed my spirit. Sports gave me something to live for outside the lab. Explore new hobbies—volunteering, hiking, reading, creative writing, etc. Whatever it is, find a hobby that will help fill some voids you might experience. Divert your energies into something that will positively impact your life.

Years later, I made peace with the loss of my brother. While writing this book, I marvel at how his loss brought tremendous changes to my life. For instance, you wouldn't be reading this book right now if not for the positive transformation that happened after I healed from my brother's loss. After wracking my brain for whom to dedicate this book to, I couldn't find anyone more deserving than him. My late brother, Joash, had an amazing outlook on life. He was always calm and seemed to have everything under control. He was a natural leader. I'm not sure if his impeccable leadership skills were innate or forced upon him as the firstborn in a big family. He also had admirable knowledge about any topic. If there were only one area in which no one rivalled him, it was his natural storytelling ability. He had a stunning way of breaking down complex topics into simple, easily understandable concepts that even a grade one pupil could grasp. Most evenings when he was home on college breaks, we would move our wooden two-legged seats around him to listen to his engrossing stories about everything from rocks in geology to the history of the Kalenjin people. He was also very good at mathematics. Most of the mathematics tricks he taught me I've never forgotten. Along with my other brothers, Joash made science and mathematics seem so much fun. It's no wonder I gravitated toward the sciences and engineering.

After graduating from college, Joash struggled to secure a well-paying job. But after not too long, he found a relatively good job and was able to provide well for his family. His life was going well. During this time, he would tell us of his monstrous dreams: how he was planning to make big investments that would earn him a good stream of income so he could retire in his early forties. He was focused, dedicated, and a go-getter, so I was certain he would make his dreams come true. Then one fine day in July 2017, my beloved brother passed away. When my housemates broke the heart-breaking news to me at Oxford, I was devastated. I travelled home a few days later to attend his funeral at our home in Nakuru County in Kenya. During his funeral, as Joash was lowered into a perfectly excavated grave hole, inch by inch, and sombre music penetrated the thick cloud of grief in the air, I couldn't help but think back to the dreams he had held and that he never got to realise his dreams. On that day, I was not only mourning my brother but also mourning his astoundingly bold dreams that never saw the light of day.

My brother died at just thirty-eight years old. All the dreams he'd planned to realise in his mid-forties died with him. Until then, I had never given death a serious thought. I knew people died. I had lost relatives before. My friends had lost close family members and I had watched them grieve. But I had never experienced death in my immediate family. Joash's death brought a sense of urgency into my life. The real and raw realisation that our thirtieth, fortieth, fiftieth, etc. birthdays are never guaranteed scared me. I began to appreciate life more, and I made a conscious decision to start working on realising my dreams, one at a time, as early as possible, whenever possible. I had pushed aside most of my big dreams (writing books, travelling, and starting business ventures) to wait for me in my forties or fifties. But my brother's death completely changed that: the realisation that my forties, fifties, sixties, etc. are not promised has pushed me to use what I have, where I am to attempt to realise my dreams, one at a time. In November 2020, as I mentioned earlier, my co-author, Elisha, and I published a book. The book is, of course, incomplete because the story of my life is still being written, but I am happy that I have published some part of my story. The book you are reading now is my second book.

I've never considered myself a writer, philanthropist, or entrepreneur, but the constant thought of dying with my dreams makes me shudder. This realisation incessantly nudges me to step forward and take baby steps towards whatever dreams I may have. I wish we knew how much time we had left in our lives so we could plan our dreams. But we don't. It might help, whenever possible, as early as possible, to start scratching the surface of our dreams. The late Paul Kalanithi, in his acclaimed memoir *When Breath Becomes Air*, writes poignantly about how he couldn't live to see all his dreams come true:

> My life had been building potential, potential that would now go unrealized. I had planned to do so much, and I had come so close. I was physically debilitated, my imagined future and my personal identity collapsed.... The lung cancer diagnosis was confirmed. My carefully planned and hard-won future no longer existed.[40]

4.14 The end of the PhD journey: Writing your thesis and preparing for viva voce

Everything that has a beginning has an end. You started this journey and you've worked diligently every step of the way. There have been high moments and low moments. Nonetheless, you've thrived and excelled. You're now at the last kilometre of your PhD race. You can see the finish line ahead of you, and exciting opportunities exuberantly await you at the finish line. But the challenge now is to cross that finish line—the crucial part of the race. How will the world know you have crossed the finish line of your PhD journey? Because you produced a big report called a thesis and successfully defended it. As I've noted before, the exact number and order of these PhD milestones will vary from one university/research field to another. But in most cases, you'll be required to produce a doctoral thesis (called a dissertation in some parts of the world). The thesis is an original document telling the world what you've been doing for the last 2-10 years. It should answer questions like: Why was the topic worth researching? How did you design and set up your experiments? What did you find out? What are the implications of your findings? What are your recommendations for future work?

As you prepare your thesis, the following tips might be helpful:

1. **Take consistent short breaks.** You'll be tempted to write your thesis all through nights and weekends. But to ensure you don't burn out, settle into a manageable work routine. Hopefully, by this time you know yourself better and how you best work. You should know if you are a night owl or a morning person and adjust your writing accordingly. Take consistent breaks. Don't forget to eat. If possible, keep engaging with your hobbies. You might want to drop some time-consuming hobbies to free up more time for writing, but still have some activities that will help reinvigorate you. Don't forget to sleep and exercise.

2. **Find a writing buddy.** Get a friend who is also working on some project, whether the target is to write a chapter, a research paper, or a thesis, so you can give each other support. Energy and motivation can be contagious. You will be able to feed off each other's motivation. Plus, your study buddy will help you be accountable, helping to drag you out of your cocoon when you don't feel like working.

3. **Anticipate delays.** So many factors outside my control delayed completing my PhD. My advisor had to read my thesis, give me feedback, and then read the final version before I had permission to officially submit it. This process took way longer than I anticipated. My viva voce was conducted by two professors in my field, one internal and one external. Getting two busy professors to agree on a common time to conduct a viva voce isn't an easy task. I submitted my thesis in September, and I hoped my viva voce would be a month after my thesis submission, but it ended up happening three months later, in December. I had secured the Schmidt Science Fellowship, and I had hoped to begin my postdoctoral fellowship in July 2019. In the end, I started my postdoctoral fellowship in April 2020. I was lucky the fellowship was flexible and allowed me ample time to wind up my PhD. As you near the end of your PhD journey and make plans for your after-PhD life, remember that some things will be out of your control, including the exact completion date. It will help to anticipate and be psychologically prepared for these probable delays. By anticipating delays, you can make plans to mitigate them. For instance, instead of waiting to complete all the chapters before submitting them to your advisor for review, as I did, maybe you could submit one completed chapter at a time as you continue to work on the rest of the chapters.

4. **Prepare sufficiently for your viva voce.** As I mentioned before, the exact number and order of PhD milestones (including viva voce) will vary from one university, department, and research field to another. Therefore, how you prepare for your viva voce will largely depend on your institution's policy on doctoral defence. Will your advisor be absent or present during your viva voce? If present, to what extent will they be allowed to help you? Is your defence written or oral? Is your defence private or public? Check and be familiar with your institution's/field's policies and practices. Your advisor can help confirm some of these policies and practices.

Below are some strategies, tips, and tricks for preparing for a viva voce. The only caveat here is that these tips and tricks are largely informed by my own experiences defending my thesis at the University of Oxford's Department of Engineering Science. But I think most of these strategies will be applicable across any other PhD field. Dedicate some time to reading some materials/ books on a PhD viva voce to get tips and tricks on how to ace your viva voce. The following books might help you understand what to expect and how to adequately prepare for the defence.

- Rowena Murray's *How to Survive Your Viva: Defending a Thesis in an Oral Examination.* I read through an information sheet from my department on what I needed to do to prepare for my viva. I also watched videos and vlogs on YouTube that gave tips on what to expect during the defence. But I still had a million questions in my mind. Only after reading this book from cover to cover and making notes did I feel fully prepared for my viva.

- Peter Smith's *The PhD Viva: How to Prepare for Your Oral Examination.* Smith, through this book, helps you understand and prepare for your oral defence. He also includes some typical defence questions and tips on how to answer them.

- Chris Marshall's *The PhD Viva Toolkit: 100 sample questions and 25+ tips to prepare you for the oral examination*. Aside from additional examples of typical defence questions, this book will also give you some insights into what examiners are looking for during your defence.

As you prepare for your viva voce, consider the following pieces of advice, inspired by Rebecca Ratcliffe's article in the *Guardian* titled "How to Survive a PhD Viva."[41]

- **Reread your thesis.** I know how tired you must feel by this stage of your research. And I also know you must have read your thesis countless times. But it's important to reread it one more time a few days before your viva to refresh your memory about the details of your research. Furthermore, rereading your thesis helps remind you of how all of your chapters tie together. While you reread your thesis, take time to scan through some recently published materials to keep up to date with new research and findings in your field.

- **Face the beast before going into viva.** List those questions you dread and hope won't be asked during your viva. With the help of your advisor and colleagues, attempt to find answers to these dreaded questions. Once you face your beast, you become more confident going into your viva. Richard Budd, a lecturer in Higher Education at Lancaster University UK, gives a long list of some common PhD viva questions in his blog.[42] They include: Why did you choose this topic? Where does your work fit into the literature? How did you develop your research questions? How did you carry out your analysis? What are the implications of your findings?

- **Eat and rest well the day before your viva.** Try to resist the strong temptation to keep reading and preparing into the night before your viva. During your viva, you'll be required to think on your feet. You'll be required to answer tough questions. Hence, you'll benefit greatly from a good sleep the night before the viva. Even better, fix a few minutes the day before to do exercises. A slow jog the day before my viva helped to calm my nerves and refresh me. All in all, treat your viva day as you would any other big day in your life. Practise whatever your big-day rituals are: meditation, exercise, etc.

- **Know by heart what your PhD contribution is.** As I mentioned earlier, what makes a thesis a PhD-level thesis is that it contributes original knowledge to your field. Therefore, you should aim to understand what an 'original contribution' in your field means. You can ask your advisor if you're unsure. In a paragraph or two, write this contribution down on a piece of paper, and discuss it with your advisor and your colleagues to make sure you know it by heart.

- **If you can, enjoy the defence.** Although this advice is akin to telling someone to enjoy a stressful job interview, despite the stress and anxiety on the day, try to enjoy the process. Remember, you have unreservedly poured lots of energy and time into your research. You have made significant contributions to your field (even if you don't exactly feel like you have during that confidence-stripping moment of your defence). So, feel proud of what you have accomplished; talk about your research confidently and with pride.

- **Be comfortable with self-doubt being your friend.** Even with the more than 10,000 hours I had poured into my research, I still had vestiges of doubt about my research abilities and my contributions. The self-doubt accompanied me up to the very second I had stepped into my viva voce. But it soon waned. After more than two hours defending my thesis, one of my examiners ended the defence saying, 'Congratulations, Dr Ngetich!" He stretched out his hand, and I shook it in disbelief. Going into the defence, I had inexorable fear. I feared there might be some gaping gaps in my thesis, or that I might not be able to sufficiently defend it. My examiner calling me 'Dr' melted some of the self-doubts I had carried with me for a while. I was officially a doctor, and it was an official stamp from my professors that I had done good work, that I had made a significant contribution to the field of jet engine cooling. And I had been officially welcomed to the prestigious select club of scholars with doctoral degrees. Although I had some minor corrections to make, I stepped out of that defence room with a new title—doctor! Confidence in my research and my contributions began to soar.

CONCLUSION
You Don't Have to Reinvent the Wheel

As Tony Robbins likes to say, "Success leaves clues." I believe we can learn a thing or two from PhD students who have striven down the PhD route and gone on to do well in their careers. Some of the clues from these predecessors will be helpful as you begin, or as you progress with your PhD. By learning from them, you'll avoid mistakes they made. Or be able just to rest in the assurance that you aren't alone when you inevitably meet occasional hurdles on the journey like doses of insecurities and fear. I asked some of my friends to briefly describe some of the things they wished they had been told before starting their PhD journeys. In their responses, you will also find some insightful thoughts and pieces of advice for prospective and ongoing PhD students. It's my deepest hope that this chapter will give you some ideas for how to start and progress along your PhD journey. Hopefully, by learning from these inspirational predecessors, you won't have to reinvent the wheel.

I will start this section by offering one thing I wish someone had told me much earlier in my life—long before I even applied to a PhD program. I wish someone had told me I didn't need an Einstein-level IQ to do a PhD. Had I known that earlier in my academic life, I would have been more confident in myself, my abilities, and my research. I would have communicated my ideas far more often and more confidently without feeling like I wasn't intelligent enough.

Growing up, I lacked female role models and mentors who had gone far in education, so I never thought I would pursue a PhD. For a very long time, I assumed a PhD was reserved for the very intelligent few. I assumed I needed an above-average IQ to manage being in a PhD program. Also, I always thought a PhD was the preserve of relatively older people, mostly men. I had never met a young woman with a PhD in engineering. All through my undergrad, I barely encountered a female lecturer in our department. As American actress Elizabeth Marvel says, 'If you can see it, you can be it'. Seeing someone like you in places you dream to be in can boost your confidence. The opposite is also true: If you don't see many people like you in your dream professions, it can unconsciously dampen your aspirations. When I got the PhD offer, I was deeply worried that I didn't have what I thought it took to manage a PhD journey. In retrospect, I now realise that what you need more than anything is a curious mind. If you enjoy finding out things, searching for solutions to problems, and investigating theories to explain some phenomena, then you are likely to enjoy and thrive in a PhD journey. Certainly, the journey will be tortuous at times, with sharp uncomfortable corners and a lot of uncertainties, demanding painstaking attention to detail, but with a curious mind, a spirit of grit, and constant support from advisors and people around you, you should be able to successfully hack the process.

Below are my friends' statements about what they wish they had been told before they embarked on their PhD journeys.

Orina Masaki

1. The kindness of PhD supervisors is far more important than the specific research project. I have had opportunities to share this advice with new graduate students over the years. It remains true now as it was when I embarked on my PhD, and particularly so for students from underrepresented backgrounds. The specifics of the project, how closely aligned the research is to your interests, the fame of the lab or supervisors—those are all great. Nothing, however, surpasses the kindness of the research supervisors in ensuring success in and away from the lab.

2. It does not matter where you start from. When a colleague laughed at the fact that I was unaware of a basic methodology, one that would be expected to feature during neuroscience class 101, I was bruised. I wondered whether I was capable of embarking on a successful research scientist path without the building blocks considered essential for it. While I may not have been exposed at the University of Nairobi to a specific method of imaging the brain, I was taught some other skills that would prove crucial to graduate schoolwork at Oxford. Those included resilience and gratitude. It does not matter where you start from. Your attitude and hard work will make up for the difference within a very short time. It may require patience. It also helps to be a little bit deaf to the giggles along the way.

3. **Family.** This is not family in the traditional sense that we would define it, but rather—who would you be calling on the days when that project is just not going right? Which doors will you be knocking on when you need to break bread and share some laughter, to distract yourself from the inevitable pain of graduate school? I will forever remain indebted to the friendships at the University of Oxford that gave me family away from home. My success in my PhD was as much theirs as it was mine.

Priyanka Dhopade

1. **Mental health is very important.** Seeking counselling therapy offered by the university can be very helpful if you find your mental health is suffering. A PhD is very satisfying and rewarding, but it can be lonely and difficult, especially if you're a minority within your environment.

2. **Learning how to write a good research article/paper is a skill that can be developed.** My first paper was terrible and received poor reviews from the peer-reviewers, so I assumed I was just a bad writer and bad scientist. I wish someone had told me my writing was something I could develop and improve.

3. **Doing a PhD does *not* mean you have to pursue a career in academia!** A PhD is a stepping stone and can lead to many diverse pathways into industry, entrepreneurship, and government, as well as academia. All the skills I learned during my PhD are valuable and transferrable to many different types of jobs and sectors.

Miriam Jerotich Kilimo

1. I wish I had been told to do everything in my power to balance work and rest. I think people told me to treat my PhD like a 9-5 job, but for me, that was advice I struggled to make my reality. I wish I had been told to protect my rest

time at all costs because once you get into the thick of PhD research and writing, it's easy to find yourself doing that all the time.

2. I wish I had developed a PhD plan that would have helped me ensure I hit certain milestones every year. PhD programs in the US usually take a minimum of five years. My program has an average graduation rate that is 6.5 years. Later in my PhD career, I found a document where a previous, very successful PhD student had outlined the milestones they hit every year. For example, publishing a paper, organising a panel presentation, etc. Although I managed to hit a number of those milestones, I feel I did them much later. I would have benefited from having a PhD plan from the onset, then doing a check-in every six months to a year.

3. I wish I had been told to have a life outside of the PhD. I think it's easy to have the entire PhD process define you. You describe yourself to others based on what your research is. Your work becomes your entire identity. I wish I had been told to pursue other hobbies just as passionately. I love writing fiction, but balancing writing fiction and doing my PhD work has been difficult for me. I wish I had been told to value my identity as a fiction writer just as much as I value my identity as a PhD researcher. Basically, find a hobby that has nothing to do with your PhD work and commit to it. It will be a welcome, refreshing outlet when things inevitably get tough during the PhD.

Suhas Mahesh

1. Only take on projects that the supervisor and the student are both excited by. Otherwise, it's like running a one-legged race; it always ends badly.

2. The world is much larger than the bit of hyper-specialised science you think about every day. Spend time thinking

about how your work connects to other developments in science, to society, to the economy, and to the future of humanity.

3. Sooner or later, we tend to become like the people around us. So, make sure to surround yourself with people you admire because you'll slowly become like them.

Javier Stober

1. I wish I had been stubborn about working on projects I was interested in, rather than what the professor pushed me towards.

2. I wish I had worked hard to get out of my research bubble and make friends across the university.

3. Impostor syndrome is real, and nearly everyone I know endured it.

Alex Kirui

1. Earning a PhD is like being thrown into the wilderness and having to find your way out. Sometimes you'll smile and sometimes you'll cry. Sometimes you'll feel smart, and most of the time you'll feel stupid. It's okay to feel this way, but it shouldn't scare you.

2. Don't be afraid to ask for help. It's normal not to know the very basic stuff; we all have different backgrounds.

3. Data and results will discourage you (most of the time). Learn to stay motivated.

Cephas Samende

1. Choose a supervisor wisely. The timely and successful completion of a PhD depends on your relationship with your supervisor. A good supervisor will help you enjoy the PhD journey. A bad supervisor can make your PhD life miserable.

2. Treat a PhD like a job. This helps to properly manage time and balance other life activities with studies.

3. Create a network of friends/colleagues and maintain communication with family. A PhD has good and bad moments. A network of friends/colleagues is helpful for moral support and informal advice on your studies and research. Family is helpful for encouragement and motivation.

Mercy Nyamewaa Asiedu

1. Who you choose as an advisor can make or break your PhD.

2. A PhD is a marathon, not a sprint. It can take 4-6 years. Take care of your mental health, and pace yourself so you make it to the finish line. Going hard too soon and too fast can lead to burnout.

3. Surround yourself with a support group; you will need them.

Ndjodi Ndeunyema

1. Trust the process.

2. Don't neglect your physical and mental health.

3. Find friends to help you cope.

122 The PhD Journey

Marion Ouma

1. Start writing early.

2. Believe in yourself. (As the proverb goes: When you see lizards crawling, you can't tell which one has a stomach-ache.)

3. Read widely.

Xiangkun (Elvis) Cao

1. Spend more time on publishing and getting professional training in scientific publishing and popular science.

2. Learn how to make better graphs and illustrations. This will be important in publishing and presentations.

3. Make valuable connections with more faculty members and peers at your university and beyond.

Contributor Biographies

1. **Orina Masaki**

   Dr Masaki is a Psychiatrist at Harvard Medical School. Prior to his current role, he was a postdoctoral fellow at the Harvard T. H. Chan School of Public Health. He has a DPhil in Neuroscience from the University of Oxford, UK. He obtained his medical degree from the University of Nairobi, Kenya.

   LinkedIn: http://www.linkedin.com/in/charlesmasaki

2. **Priyanka Dhopade**

   Dr Dhopade is an Assistant Professor at the University of Auckland, New Zealand. She has a PhD in Aerospace Engineering, UNSW Canberra, Australia, and a MEng in Aerospace Engineering from Monash University, Australia. She obtained her BEng in Aerospace Engineering from Ryerson University, Canada.

   Twitter: @drpriaero

3. **Miriam Jerotich Kilimo**

   Kilimo is a PhD student in Anthropology, Emory, USA. She has an MSt in Women's Studies from the University of Oxford, UK, and an MA in Anthropology from Emory University, USA. She obtained her BA in Anthropology Modified and Senior Fellow from Dartmouth College, USA.

   Personal website: miriamjerotich.com

4. **Suhas Mahesh**

   Dr Mahesh is a Visiting Researcher at the University of Oxford, UK. He has a DPhil in Condensed Matter Physics from the University of Oxford, and a BSc in Physics from the Indian Institute of Science, India.

   Twitter: @suhasm

5. **Javier Stober**

   Dr Stober is a Research Engineer at MIT Media Lab, USA. He has a master's degree and PhD both in Aeronautics and Astronautics from Stanford University, USA. He obtained a dual undergraduate degree in Mechanical Engineering and Aerospace Engineering from the University of Florida, USA.

   LinkedIn: www.linkedin.com/in/javier-stober/

6. **Alex Kirui**

   Kirui is a PhD student at Louisiana State University and a Summer Intern at Boehringer Ingelheim Pharmaceuticals, USA. He obtained his BTech, Industrial Chemistry from the Technical University of Kenya, Kenya.

   Twitter: @kipalexkip
   LinkedIn: www.linkedin.com/in/alex-kirui-36895380/

7. **Cephas Samende**

   Dr Samende is a Postdoctoral Research Associate at Keele University, UK. He has a DPhil in Engineering Science from the University of Oxford, UK, and a BEng in Electrical and Electronics Engineering from the University of Zambia, Zambia.

   LinkedIn: www.linkedin.com/in/csamende/

8. **Mercy Nyamewaa Asiedu**

   Dr Asiedu is a Postdoctoral Fellow at MIT. She is the co-founder of GAPhealth Technologies and Calla Health Foundation. She has a PhD in Biomedical Engineering and an MSc in Biomedical Engineering, both from Duke University, USA. She obtained her BSc in Biomedical Engineering (Business Minor) from the University of Rochester, USA.

   LinkedIn: www.linkedin.com/in/mercy-n-asiedu/

9. **Ndjodi Ndeunyema**

   Dr Ndeunyema is a trainee lawyer in the UK. He has a DPhil in Law from the University of Oxford, UK. He has an MSc, a BCL, and an MPhil in Law from the University of Oxford, United Kingdom. He obtained an LLB from the University of Namibia, Namibia.

   Personal Website: www.ndjodi.com

10. **Marion Ouma**

    Dr Ouma is a Research Fellow at the University of South Africa, South Africa. She has a PhD in Sociology from the University of South Africa, South Africa. She obtained both her Master of Arts and Bachelor of Arts from the University of Nairobi, Kenya.

    Twitter: @MarionOuma

11. **Xiangkun (Elvis) Cao**

    Dr Cao is a Postdoctoral Researcher at MIT, USA. He has an MS and a PhD in Mechanical Engineering from Cornell University, USA, and an MEng (Thesis) in Materials Engineering from McGill University, Canada. He obtained his BEng in Energy and Power Engineering, and his BA in English Language and Literature from Xi'an Jiaotong University, China.

Twitter: @Elvis_Cao
Personal Website: elviscao.com

12. Mercy Akoth

Akoth is a Senior Consultant, Ernst & Young, UK. She has an MSc in Statistical Sciences and an MBA, both from the University of Oxford, UK. She obtained her BBS in Actuarial Science from Strathmore University, Kenya.

LinkedIn: www.linkedin.com/inmercy-akoth-fia-101091147/

13. Rono Kipkorir

Kipkorir is a Senior Technologist at Jomo Kenyatta University of Agriculture and Technology, Kenya. He has an MSc in Vehicle Engineering from Wuhan University and Technology in China. He obtained his BSc in Mechanical Engineering from Jomo Kenyatta University of Agriculture and Technology, Kenya.

Twitter: @markipkorir
Facebook: Rono Kipkorir

14. Godfrey Marambe

Engineer Marambe is the Director of Energy Intelligence Africa. He has an MSc in Energy Management from the University of Nairobi and an MBA from the United States International University in Kenya. He obtained his BSc in Mechanical Engineering from the University of Nairobi, Kenya.

LinkedIn: https://www.linkedin.com/in/
eng-godfrey-marambe/

15. Patrick Kiprotich Korir

Korir is a Process Engineer at Höganäs AB, Sweden. He has an MSc in Materials Science from the KTH Royal Institute of Technology, Sweden. He obtained his BSc in Mechanical Engineering from Jomo Kenyatta University of Agriculture and Technology, Kenya.

Acknowledgements

This book has become a reality because of so many people. I sincerely appreciate my contributing friends for taking time out of their busy schedules to offer honest experiences and deeply-thought-out pieces of advice about their PhD journeys. No doubt their pieces of advice will be timely for both prospective and current PhD students.

Ruth Nyakerario, thank you for being my accountability partner throughout the writing of this book and always gently asking, 'No pressure, but how is your new book coming along?' I deeply appreciate your comments and suggestions for how I could make this book better. Deepest gratitude also to Ndahafa Kapani, Patrick Kiprotich, Cephas Samende, and Rono Kipkorir for your thoughtful feedback and insights on the first drafts of the manuscript. I also thank Priyanka Dhopade for writing a thoughtful foreword and Sindhu Majeti for her impressive illustrations that added character to this book.

To everyone who contributed ideas through random informal discussions and moral support, I sincerely thank you;

this book wouldn't be a success without each of you. For generous support and guiding me through the publishing journey, I would like to give special thanks to Susan Friedmann, Tyler Tichelaar, Meredith Lindsay, Jasmine Florentine, Andrea Gwosdow, and Yuki Machida.

I thank my family for the support, inspiration, and love you afforded me, not only while I was writing this book, but also through all seasons of life, bad and good. All through my PhD and post-PhD, I was miles away from home. But every time I was in touch with you, I felt your love, support, and care. My life would be less interesting without you guys.

Bibliography

Angelou, Maya. "A Day Away." *Wouldn't Take Nothing for My Journey Now*. Bantam, 2011. p. 137-139.

Bolker, Joan. *Writing Your Dissertation in Fifteen Minutes a Day: A Guide to Starting, Revising, and Finishing Your Doctoral Thesis*. New York, NY: Henry Holt, 1998.

Budd, Richard. "Is it a PhD...or not a PhD? Unpacking the viva." 15 September 2014. https://ddubdrahcir.wordpress.com/2014/09/15/is-it-a-phd-or-not-a-phd-unpacking-the-viva/. Accessed 8 February 2022.

Cao, Xiangkun (Elvis). "Flourishing as a Minority in Higher Education." https://www.lindau-nobel.org/blog-flourishing-as-a-minority-in-higher-education/. Accessed 8 February 2022.

Clear, James. *Atomic Habits: An Easy & Proven Way to Build Good Habits & Break Bad Ones*. New York, NY: Penguin, 2018.

Cornell University. "'30 Under 30' Doctoral Student Fights Climate Change by Converting Carbon Dioxide into Clean Fuel." 14 January 2019. https://medium.com/cornell-university/doctoral-student-fights-climate-change-by-converting-carbon-dioxide-into-clean-fuel-6332e0e12951. Accessed 7 February 2022.

Covey, Stephen. *The 7 Habits of Highly Effective People*. New York, NY: Simon & Schuster, 2020.

Fried, Jason and David Heinemeier Hansson. *ReWork: Change the Way You Work Forever.* New York, NY: Random House, 2010.

Gebhard, Nathan. "Four Steps to Choosing a College Major." *The New York Times.* 31 July 2015. https://www.nytimes.com/2015/08/02/education/edlife/four-steps-to-choosing-a-career-path.html. Accessed 8 February 2022.

Gewin, Virginia. "The Jet Engineer." *Nature.* 574 (2019): 590.

Grayson, Malika. *Hooded: A Black Girl's Guide to the Ph.D.* Atlanta, GA: Mynd Matters, 2020.

Heracleous, Loivos and David Robson. "Why Procrastination Can Help Fuel Creativity." 31 March 2021. https://www.bbc.com/worklife/article/20210319-why-procrastination-can-help-fuel-creativity. Accessed 8 February 2022.

Joyner, Randy L., William A. Rouse, and Allan A. Glatthorn. *Writing the Winning Thesis or Dissertation: A Step-by-Step Guide.* Thousand Oaks, CA: SAGE Publications, 2012.

Karp, Jason. *How to Survive Your PhD: The Insider's Guide to Avoiding Mistakes, Choosing the Right Program, Working with Professors, and Just How a Person Actually Writes a 200-Page Paper.* Naperville, IL: Sourcebooks, 2009.

Khazan, Olga. "The Upside of Pessimism." *The Atlantic.* September 2014. https://www.theatlantic.com/health/archive/2014/09/dont-think-positively/379993/. Accessed 7 February 2022.

Knight, Phil. *Shoe Dog: A Memoir by the Creator of Nike.* New York, NY: Simon and Schuster, 2016.

Lamott, Ann. "12 Truths I Learned from Life and Writing." https://www.ted.com/talks/anne_lamott_12_truths_i_learned_from_life_and_writing?language=en. Accessed 7 February 2022.

Lightman, Alan. *In Praise of Wasting Time.* New York, NY: Simon & Schuster/TED, 2018.

Marshall, Chris. *The PhD Viva Toolkit: 100 sample questions and 25+ tips to prepare you for the oral examination.* n.p.: independently published, 2019.

Masello, Robert. *Robert's Rules of Writing, Second Edition: 111 Unconventional Lessons That Every Writer Needs to Know.* New York, NY: Simon and Schuster, 2021.

Maslow, Abraham. "Building a Firm-Wide Sales Capability." *Method Grid.* 22 January 2018. https://methodgrid.com/blog/10-building-a-firm-wide-sales-capability/. Accessed 25 February 2022.

Murray, Rowena. *How to Survive Your Viva: Defending a Thesis in an Oral Examination.* Maidenhead, Gr. Brit.: McGraw-Hill Education, 2015.

Murray, Rowena. *How to Write a Thesis.* Maidenhead, Gr. Brit.: McGraw-Hill Education, 2011.

Newport, Cal. *Deep Work: Rules for Focused Success in a Distracted World.* New York, NY: Grand Central Publishing, 2016.

Ngetich, Gladys Chepkirui and Elisha Kipkemoi Ngetich. *The Bold Dream: Transcending the Impossible.* n.p.: New Generation Publishing, 2020.

Ratcliffe, Rebecca. "How to Survive a PhD Viva: 17 Top Tips." *The Guardian*. 8 January 2015. https://www.theguardian.com/ higher-education-network/2015/jan/08/how-to-survive-a-phd-viva-17-top-tips. Accessed 25 February 2022.

Robinson, Ken. "Do Schools Kill Creativity?" *TED*. 2006. https://www.ted.com/talks/sir_ken_robinson_do_schools_kill_ creativity. Accessed 7 February 2022.

Schlesinger, Leonard A., Charles F. Kiefer, and Paul B. Brown. *Just Start: Take Action, Embrace Uncertainty, Create the Future*. Cambridge, MA: Harvard Business Press, 2012.

Schramm, J. D. *Communicate with Mastery: Speak With Conviction and Write for Impact*. Hoboken, NJ: John Wiley & Sons, 2020.

Smith, Peter. *The PhD Viva: How to Prepare for Your Oral Examination*. New York, NY: Palgrave MacMillan, 2014.

The Guardian staff reporter. "How Not to Get a PhD." *The Guardian*. 7 November 2002. https://www.theguardian.com/ education/2002/nov/08/highereducation.books. Accessed 25 February 2022.

Tracy, Brian. *Master Your Time, Master Your Life: The Breakthrough System to Get More Results, Faster, in Every Area of Your Life*. New York, NY: Penguin, 2016.

Valadez-Martinez, Laura. "Things About a PhD Nobody Told You About." TEDxLoughboroughU. 2016. https://www.youtube.com/watch?v=CAKsQf77nHU. Accessed 7 February 2022.

Endnotes

1 Covey p. 113.
2 Karp p. 37.
3 https://www.ox.ac.uk/admissions/graduate/courses/ dphil-engineering-science.
4 Grayson p. 39.
5 Ibid. p. 43.
6 Newport p. 253.
7 Karp p. 33.
8 Grayson p. 71.
9 https://www.nytimes.com/2015/08/02/education/edlife/four-steps-to-choosing-a-career-path.html
10 https://medium.com/cornell-university/doctoral-student-fights-climate-change-by-converting-carbon-dioxide-into-clean-fuel-6332e0e12951.
11 https://www.lindau-nobel.org/ blog-flourishing-as-a-minority-in-higher-education/.
12 https://www.nytimes.com/2015/08/02/education/edlife/four-steps-to-choosing-a-career-path.html
13 Clear p. 171.
14 Grayson p. 74.
15 https://www.theguardian.com/education/2002/nov/08/higher education.books.
16 Masello p. 209.
17 Ibid. p. 17.

About the Author

Gladys Chepkirui Ngetich is a Rhodes Scholar and a Schmidt Science Fellow. She is currently working as a Postdoctoral Fellow at the Space Enabled Research Group at MIT. She earned her DPhil in Engineering Science at the University of Oxford. Before joining Oxford, Gladys pursued her bachelor's degree in mechanical engineering at Jomo Kenyatta University of Agriculture and Technology in Kenya.

Gladys has been a recipient of many notable awards and recognitions, including the International Astronautical Federation Emerging Space Leader Award, International Gas Turbine Institute Young Engineer Award, UK Rare Rising Star, Skoll World Forum Fellowship, and Kenya's Top 40 Under 40 Women. Gladys' research and her inspirational academic journey have been featured in *Nature* and twice on *BBC Science News*.

Scan this code to discover more about Gladys.

Website: www.gladyschepkirui.com

LinkedIn: www.linkedin.com/in/gladyscngetich/

Twitter: @gladys_ngetich

Facebook: facebook.com/gladys.chepkirui.ngetich/

Printed in Great Britain
by Amazon

81069000R00079

18 https://www.ted.com/talks/anne_lamott_12_truths_i_learned_from_life_and_writing?language=en.

19 Masello p. 152.

20 Clear p. 142.

21 Cited in Khazan. https://www.theatlantic.com/health/archive/2014/09/dont-think-positively/379993/.

22 Knight p. 5.

23 https://www.goodreads.com/quotes/177079-convince-yourself-that-you-are-working-in-clay-not-marble.

24 Robinson. https://www.ted.com/talks/sir_ken_robinson_do_schools_kill_creativity.

25 https://methodgrid.com/blog/10-building-a-firm-wide-sales-capability/.

26 Heracleous and Robson. https://www.bbc.com/worklife/article/20210319-why-procrastination-can-help-fuel-creativity.

27 Angelou p. 139.

28 Lightman p. 73.

29 Angelou p. 27.

30 Covey p. 342.

31 Tracy p. 194.

32 Newport p. 3.

33 Tracy p. 193.

34 Valadez-Martinez. https://www.youtube.com/watch?v=CAKsQf77nHU.

35 Gewin p. 590.

36 Schramm p. 129.

37 Karp p. 146.

38 Clear p. 81.

39 Ibid. p. 84.

40 Kalanithi p. 120.

41 https://www.theguardian.com/higher-education-network/2015/jan/08/how-to-survive-a-phd-viva-17-top-tips.

42 https://ddubdrahcir.wordpress.com/2014/09/15/is-it-a-phd-or-not-a-phd-unpacking-the-viva/